Arthur and the Minimoys

Luc Besson is the internationally-renowned and award-winning writer/director/producer behind such movies as *The Fifth Element*, *Nikita*, *Léon* and *The Big Blue*. *Arthur and the Minimoys* is his first novel for young readers, soon to be followed by the sequel, *Arthur and the Forbidden City*. He is currently working on a film based on both books, which will be released in 2006.

Coming soon from Luc Besson
Arthur and the Forbidden City

LUC BESSON

ARTHUR
AND THE
MINIMOYS

From an original idea by Céline Garcia

Translated by Ellen Sowchek

First published in France in 2002
as 'Arthur et les Minimoys'
by Intervista

First published in the UK in 2005
by Faber & Faber Limited
3 Queen Square London WC1N 3AU

Typeset by Faber and Faber Limited
Printed in England by Mackays of Chatham plc, Chatham, Kent

A CIP record for this book
is available from the British Library

ISBN 0–571–22604–3

2 4 6 8 10 9 7 5 3 1

Arthur and the Minimoys

Chapter 1

The landscape was green and gently rolling, grazed closely by the hot sun. Above it the sky was blue, filled with small cotton-wool clouds.

It was quiet, as were all of the mornings during this long summer vacation, when even the birds seemed lazy.

In the middle of the peaceful valley was a small garden by a river that flowed past an unusual-looking house. It had a long balcony and was made entirely of wood. To one side stood a large garage with a huge wooden water tank perched on top.

An old windmill kept watch over the garden, much like a lighthouse watches over its boats. It seemed to turn just for the fun of it. In this little corner of paradise, even the wind blew gently.

Nothing on this beautiful morning hinted at the terrible adventure that was about to begin.

*

The front door exploded open. A large woman filling the entryway. 'ARTHUR!' she yelled, in a voice that could make glass shatter.

Grandma was about sixty years old and rather round, even though her elegant black dress, trimmed with lace, was designed to hide her plumpness.

She finished putting on her gloves, adjusted her hat, and yanked violently on the ancient doorbell. 'Arthur!' she yelled again. No answer.

'Where on earth is that boy? And the dog! Has Alfred disappeared, too?' Grandma grumbled like a distant storm as she went back into the house.

Inside, the wooden floor gleamed with polish, and lace seemed to have conquered all of the furniture, the way that ivy takes over walls.

Grandma put on her house slippers and crossed the room, muttering, '"An excellent watchdog, you'll see!" How did I ever fall for that?'

She huffed up the stairs.

'I wonder what exactly he's watching, this "watch-dog"! He's never *in* the house to watch it! He and Arthur just breeze through!' she grumbled, opening the door to Arthur's bedroom. Still no sign of Arthur.

'Do you think it bothers them that their poor grandmother must run after them all day long? Not at all!' She continued down the hall. 'I don't ask for much – only that he keep still for just five minutes a day, like other ten-year-olds!' Suddenly she paused, struck by a thought. She listened to the house, which was unusually silent.

Grandma began to speak in a low voice.

'Five minutes of peace . . . when he could play calmly . . . in a corner . . . without making any noise . . .' she murmured, gliding towards the end of the hallway. She reached the last door, on which hung a wooden sign engraved with the words KEEP OUT.

She opened the door quietly and peered into the forbidden room.

It was an attic that had been converted into a large office, resembling a cross between a merry antique shop and the study of a slightly nutty professor. On either side of the desk were large bookshelves overflowing with leather-bound books. Hanging above it all was a silk banner on which a cryptic message was printed: WORDS OFTEN HIDE OTHER WORDS. Our scholar was also a philosopher.

Grandma moved slowly into the middle of the bric-a-brac, all of which had a decidedly African flavour. Around the room spears seemed to have pushed through the floor like shoots of bamboo. A fantastic collection of African masks hung on the wall. They were magnificent . . . except for the one that was missing. A lone, telltale nail stuck out of the wall.

Aha! Grandma had her first clue. All she had to do now was follow the snores that were becoming more and more audible.

Grandma moved farther into the room and, sure enough, discovered Arthur stretched out on the floor, the African mask on his face amplifying his snores. Alfred, of course, was stretched out alongside him, his tail beating time on the wooden mask.

Grandma couldn't help but smile.

'You could at least answer when I call you! I've been looking for you for almost an hour!' she murmured to the dog, speaking quietly so as not to wake Arthur too suddenly.

Alfred gave his best cute and innocent look.

'Oh, don't give me that puppy-dog face! You know I don't want you in Grandpa's room and you're not allowed to touch his things!' she said firmly, reaching to lift the mask from Arthur's face.

In the light, he had the face of a naughty angel. Grandma melted like snow in the sun. She breathed a happy sigh at the sight of the sleeping boy who lit up her life.

Alfred whined a little – perhaps out of jealousy.

'That's enough out of you, Alfred! If I were you, I would make myself scarce for the next five minutes,' she said sternly. Alfred took the hint and backed off. Grandma lovingly placed her hand on the boy's face.

'Arthur?' she murmured. The snoring only became louder.

She changed her tone.

'Arthur!' she thundered, her voice echoing through the room. The boy jumped up with a start, bewildered and ready for battle.

'Help! An attack! Quick, men! Alfred! Form a circle!' he shouted, half asleep. Grandma grabbed his shoulders.

'Arthur, calm down! It's me! It's Grandma!' she barked. Arthur shook himself awake and realized who he was facing.

'Oh, sorry, Grandma. I was in Africa.'

'I can see that!' she replied with a smile. 'Did you have a good trip?'

'Fantastic! I was with Grandpa and a whole African tribe. They were friends of his,' he added helpfully.

Grandma played along. 'Oh, my. What happened?'

'We were surrounded by dozens of ferocious lions that came out of nowhere!'

'My goodness! What did you do to escape?' she asked, pretending to sound worried.

'Me, nothing,' he replied modestly. 'It was Grandpa who did everything. He unrolled a large cloth and we hung it up, right in the middle of the savannah!'

'A cloth? What kind of a cloth?' asked Grandma, mystified.

Arthur was already up and climbing on a crate to reach the top shelf. He took down a book and opened it quickly to the right page.

'There, see, like this! He painted a canvas that he hung in a circle around us. That way, the wild animals saw only the painted scenery, so they turned away and couldn't find us. It was as if we were . . . invisible,' he concluded with satisfaction.

'Invisible, perhaps, but not odourless!' Grandma responded.

Arthur stared at her blankly.

'Did you take your shower this morning?' she asked.

'Well, I was about to, but then I found this book! And it was so interesting that I forgot everything else,' he confessed, leafing through the pages. 'Look at all these drawings! This is the work that Grandpa did for the most isolated tribes. Hardly anyone else has ever seen or heard of them.'

Grandma glanced down at the drawings, which she knew by heart.

'What I see is that he was more interested in African tribes than in his own,' she replied with a smile.

Arthur was immersed in the drawings. 'Look at this one. He dug a super-deep well and invented an entire system with bamboo to transport water more than a mile away!'

'It's ingenious, I know, but to be fair the Romans invented that system long before he did. They are called pipelines,' Grandma reminded him.

This was a page of history that Arthur had totally missed.

'The Romans? I've never heard of that tribe!' he said.

Grandma smiled. 'It was a very old tribe that lived in Italy a long time ago,' she explained. 'Their chief was named Caesar.'

'Like the salad?' Arthur asked.

'Yes, like the salad,' replied Grandma, smiling once again. 'Come on, let's straighten up. We have to go into town to do some shopping.'

'Does that mean no shower today?' asked Arthur with delight.

'No, it just means no shower right now! You can take one when we get back! Now hurry up!' Grandma ordered.

Arthur carefully rearranged the books that he had scattered while Grandma put back the African mask. They had a proud look, all these warriors' masks, which had been given to her husband as a sign of friendship by various tribes. Grandma gazed at them a moment, remembering the adventures that she had shared with her husband, who had been missing now for four long years.

Nostalgia overwhelmed her and she let out a deep sigh, as long as a memory.

'Grandma – why did Grandpa leave?'

The question resonated in the silence. She glanced over at Arthur, who was staring up at the portrait of Grandpa in his helmet and full colonial garb.

Grandma searched for the right words. She always had trouble when emotion was too close to the surface. She moved towards the open window and took a deep breath.

'That, Arthur, is something I would really like to know . . .' she answered, closing the window. She remained there for an instant, looking down at the garden. An old garden gnome smiled up at her from the foot of an imposing oak that overlooked the place.

How many memories had this old oak accumulated during its lifetime? It could probably tell this story better than anyone, but it was Grandma who continued.

'Grandpa spent a lot of time in his garden, near that old oak tree that he loved so much. He said that it was three hundred years older than he was, and so it must have a lot of things to teach him.'

Without making a sound, Arthur perched on the edge of a chair, anticipating a story.

'I can still picture him at nightfall, with his telescope, observing the stars,' recounted Grandma in a soft voice. 'The full moon was shining. It was . . . magnificent. I could watch him for hours when he was like that – passionate, fluttering like a butterfly excited by the light.' Grandma smiled, replaying the scene in her memory. Then her smile faded and her face grew hard.

'And then one morning, both he and the telescope were gone. Disappeared. That was almost four years ago.'

Arthur was a bit stunned. 'He disappeared just like that? Without a word, a note – without anything?'

Grandma nodded sadly. 'It must have been something very important for him to leave like that, without telling us,' she said with a touch of humour.

She clapped her hands as if she were popping a soap bubble to break a magic spell.

'Come on! We're going to be late! Go put on your jacket!'

Arthur ran happily towards his room. Only children seem to have this ability to shift so quickly from one emotion to another, as if the heaviest things do not really have any weight before the age of ten. Grandma smiled at this thought. For her, it was often difficult to forget the weight of things, even if only for a few minutes.

Grandma adjusted her hat one more time. She crossed the front garden towards her faithful old Chevrolet pick-up.

Arthur wriggled into his jacket as he ran up to the

passenger side. A trip in this vehicle was like a journey on an antiquated spaceship, worthy of space pioneers – always an adventure.

Grandma fiddled with two or three buttons and turned the key, which was as stubborn as a stuck door-knob. The motor coughed, crackled, then raced, jammed, became blocked, cleared itself, revved up, and finally started.

Arthur loved the hum of the old diesel engine, which sounded very much like a manic washing machine.

Alfred the dog, on the other hand, kept his distance from the truck, as if he couldn't understand why there needed to be all this noise for so little result.

Grandma addressed him through the window:

'Excuse me, Alfred. Would it be possible, if it's not too much trouble, for you to do me a very big favour?'

The dog lifted one ear. He knew well that favours were often associated with rewards.

'Watch this house!' she ordered.

The dog barked, not really sure what he was agreeing to.

'Thank you. That is very kind of you,' Grandma responded. She released the emergency brake, shifted the Chevrolet into gear, and rolled towards the road.

A cloud of dust bloomed in the slight wind that blew over the countryside. The truck travelled over the green hills, taking the small, twisting road to civilization, or the nearest thing to it.

The town was not big but it was very pleasant. Almost all of the shops and merchants could be found on the wide main street.

Grandma parked in front of a store that, without a doubt, was the largest in the town. An imposing sign announced the name of the owner and its purpose:

DAVIDO CORPORATION – FOOD SUPPLIERS

Which meant that it covered a lot.

Arthur liked going to the supermarket. It was the most modern store in this friendly little town, the closest thing he had to a space station. And, since he imagined himself to be travelling by spaceship, there was a certain logic to his thoughts, even if it was a logic that only children could comprehend.

Grandma primped a little before she got out of the car, knowing she would run into her friend Martin, the police officer.

Martin was around forty years old, rather jovial, with hair that was already turning grey. He had the look of a cocker spaniel but a smile that saved everything.

He hurried over and opened the supermarket door for Grandma.

'Thank you, officer,' said Grandma politely, pleased by his gentlemanliness.

'You're welcome, Mrs Suchot. It is always a pleasure to see you in town,' he added.

'It is always a pleasure to run into you here, officer,' replied Grandma, happy to play along.

Martin twisted his hat in his hands, as if he had run out of conversation.

'Do you need anything out there? Is everything all right?'

'Well, there's no lack of chores, but it certainly prevents boredom! And then I have my little Arthur. It's nice to have a man around the house,' she added, ruffling her grandson's hair.

Arthur hated it when people patted him on the head. It made him feel like a stuffed toy. He pulled away with a frown, and this was all it took to make Martin even more nervous and awkward.

'And . . . the dog that my brother sold you? Is he working out well?'

'Better than that! He's a real beast!' Grandma said with a chuckle. 'Fortunately my little Arthur, who knows so much about Africa, was able to tame him, thanks to the techniques he learned there,' she said. 'The animal is now well trained, even though we know that the wild beast is still sleeping inside him. Sleeping rather a lot, in fact,' she added teasingly.

'Good, good – I am delighted,' Martin stammered, as if he were not quite sure this was the right thing to say. He continued regretfully, 'Yes, well . . . goodbye, Mrs S.'

'Goodbye, officer,' Grandma replied with a friendly

nod. Martin watched them pass and gently let go of the door, the way one lets go of a sigh.

Arthur used all of his strength to separate two shopping carts, which were evidently madly in love with each other.

He found his grandmother already in one of the four aisles, shopping list in hand.

Arthur let his feet slide to slow down his cart. He moved close to his grandmother in order not to be overheard by anyone else.

'Grandma, wasn't that police officer flirting with you just a little?' he said bluntly.

'Arthur! Where did you learn that word?' she asked.

'Well, it's true, isn't it? As soon as he sees you, he starts strutting like a duck and acting as if he is going to eat his hat. Mrs S. this, Mrs S. that!'

'Arthur! Stop!' Grandma said. 'Let's have some decorum. We do not speak about people by comparing them to ducks.'

Arthur shrugged. He wasn't convinced that he'd been rude. All he'd done was point out the truth.

Grandma calmed down. 'He is very nice to me, as is everyone in the village,' she explained in a serious voice. 'Your grandfather was well liked here, because he helped people with his inventions, just as he did in the villages in Africa. And when he disappeared, people like Martin were a great comfort to me.'

The conversation had turned sombre. Arthur felt it and stopped squirming.

'Believe me, without their kindness, I would probably not have been able to stand the loneliness,' Grandma admitted.

Arthur remained silent. You don't always know what to say, and that's true whether you are ten years old or a hundred.

Grandma patted his head affectionately and handed him the shopping list.

'Here. I'll let you do the rest. I know you like to. I have to go find something at Mrs Rosenberg's. If you finish before I do, wait for me at the checkout.'

Arthur nodded, already delighted at the prospect of travelling the aisles aboard his iron vessel on wheels.

'Can I buy some straws?' he asked.

Grandma gave him a big smile.

'Of course, dear. As many as you like.'

That was all he needed to hear. He set off down the aisle with a grin.

Grandma left the store and crossed the main street, being careful to look right and left even if it wasn't absolutely necessary, given the rather light traffic in this town. Perhaps it was a reflex from an earlier time, when she and her husband had travelled in the great capitals of Europe and Africa. She entered the Rosenbergs' small hardware store, where even the doorbell had a story all its own. She was on a mission. It was Arthur's birthday and she had planned a special surprise.

Mrs Rosenberg appeared, popping out like a jack-in-the-box. She had been at the window for an hour, waiting for her friend to arrive.

'He didn't follow you, did he?' she asked, too excited to say hello.

Grandma gave a quick glance back over her shoulder. 'No, I don't think so. I don't think he suspects anything.'

'Perfect! Perfect!' The merchant bounced as she went back into the store. She bent behind the imposing counter, took out a package wrapped in brown paper, and placed it delicately on the old wood surface.

'Here you are. Everything's there,' she said with a smile that made her look as if she were five years old.

'Thank you. You are wonderful. You cannot know how you have helped me with my surprise. How much do I owe you?'

'What do you think? Nothing! I had a great time!'

Grandma was caught off guard, and her excellent upbringing forced her to insist, 'Mrs Rosenberg, that is very kind, but I cannot accept.'

Mrs Rosenberg was already handing her the package.

'Go on, don't argue, and hurry before he suspects something!' She hustled her friend to the door.

The two old ladies exchanged knowing smiles.

'Go on, out with you!' said Mrs Rosenberg. 'And I am counting on you to stop by tomorrow and tell me everything in the smallest detail.'

Grandma agreed with a smile. 'I won't forget. See you tomorrow.'

'See you tomorrow,' said the hardware dealer, returning to her observation post at the corner of the window. Outside, Grandma opened the Chevrolet door and slipped the mysterious package under the seat.

When Grandma met Arthur at the checkout counter at Davido's, he was already emptying the contents of the cart onto the rolling belt, arranging everything in little trains, alternating pasta and toothpaste, sugar and apple shampoo, a packet of straws.

'You found everything?' Grandma asked.

'Yes, yes,' replied Arthur, absorbed by the arrangements.

A second packet of straws passed under Grandma's nose.

'I was afraid you wouldn't be able to read my writing.'

'No problem. And did you find what you were looking for?'

Grandma experienced a moment of panic. Lying to a child can be the most difficult thing in the world.

'Yes . . . uh . . . no. In fact – it wasn't ready. Next week, maybe,' she stammered, nervously filling the first bag with packets of straws. She was so distracted that it wasn't until the sixth packet of one hundred straws that she finally reacted.

'Arthur! What on earth are you doing with all these straws?'

'You said I could get as many as I wanted, didn't you?'

'Yes, but . . . that was just a figure of speech.'

'Well, that's the last one!' he said with a charming grin. Grandma was at a loss for words.

The old Chevrolet, more tired now than during the trip into town, was parked near the kitchen window, where it was easier to unload the groceries.

Arthur began to pile packages on the window ledge.

'I'll do that,' Grandma said. 'Go play while it is still daylight.'

Arthur didn't argue. He grabbed his bagful of straws and ran off barking – or, no, that was Alfred, chasing after him with equal joy. Grandma was now able to remove her mysterious package unseen and sneak it quietly into the house.

Arthur turned on the long fluorescent light in the garage, which crackled a bit before lighting up the room. Out of habit, he grabbed a dart near the door and sent it flying to the opposite side of the room. Bull's-eye!

'Yes!' he cried, waving his arms in a victory sign.

He crossed the room to the workbench, which was

littered with bits and pieces of a strange contraption. It consisted of several pieces of bamboo carefully cut lengthwise and pierced with small holes all over.

Arthur enthusiastically opened each packet of straws, one by one. There were all kinds, in all sizes and colours. He hesitated before selecting the first one, the way a surgeon chooses a scalpel before beginning an operation.

He finally chose one and tried to fit it into the first hole in one of the pieces of bamboo. The hole was just a bit too small. No problem – Arthur simply took out his Swiss army knife and widened the hole. The second attempt was an immediate success. The straw fitted perfectly.

Arthur turned to his dog, the lone privileged witness to this memorable event.

'Alfred, you are about to see the greatest irrigation system in the entire region. Bigger than Caesar's, more perfect than Grandpa's, here it is: the Arthur system!'

Alfred yawned, overcome with emotion.

Arthur the builder crossed the garden, carrying his immense length of bamboo, pierced with a dozen straws, on his shoulder.

Grandma, still occupied with putting away the groceries, saw him pass by the kitchen window and was momentarily stunned. She blinked a few times, then shrugged her shoulders.

Arthur placed the bamboo on small, branched

tripods he had built for this purpose. The whole thing was perched above a carefully dug ditch at the bottom of which were small radish seedlings, regularly spaced.

He went back to the garage, found the garden hose, and began to unroll it.

So far, so good.

Arthur, under Alfred's anxious eye, attached the hose to the end of the bamboo, sticking it in place with pieces of multicoloured modelling clay. He then turned the bamboo until the straws were positioned above each seedling.

'This is the most delicate moment, Alfred,' he said, quoting from one of his grandfather's books. 'The calibration must be correct to the exact degree in order to avoid a flood or the total destruction of the crop,' he added in a serious voice, as if he were handling explosives.

Alfred didn't particularly care about radishes. He trotted off and returned with his old tennis ball, which he dropped on top of a young seedling.

'Alfred! This is really not the time!' Arthur shouted. 'And no civilians allowed on the work site!' He picked up the ball and threw it as far as possible. Alfred took this as a sign that the game had begun, and he charged off, nose to the ground, in pursuit of his prey.

While he was gone, Arthur finished his adjustments

and ran over to the tap on the wall of the garage.

The dog returned, ball in mouth, but his master had disappeared.

Arthur put his hand on the tap and turned it slowly.

'Please work!' he prayed. He took off, running alongside the hose to arrive before the stream of water.

Halfway there, he ran right past the dog, who had come in search of him. Alfred was completely bewildered by this new variation in his game, but he spun around and followed.

Arthur threw himself to the ground and followed the stream of water on all fours as it filled the bamboo and ran through the straws one by one.

Each young radish seedling was happily watered. Alfred put down his ball, intrigued by this machine that could pee on all the flowers at once.

'Yes!' shouted Arthur, grabbing his dog's paw and pumping it up and down cheerfully. 'Congratulations! This is a remarkable work that shall be remembered by history, believe me!' he said, speaking for Alfred.

Grandma appeared on the porch, an apron around her waist.

'Arthur! Telephone!' she yelled. Arthur let go of his dog's paw.

'Excuse me, Alfred. It is probably the president of the water company calling to congratulate me. I will be back in a minute.'

Chapter 2

Arthur was so excited as he entered the living room that he managed, in his socks, to cross the entire room in a single slide.

He grabbed the phone and nestled deep into the comfortable couch.

'I made an irrigation system, just like Caesar! But in my case, it's for *making* salads! It's to help Grandma's radishes grow! With my system, they will grow twice as fast!' he shouted into the telephone without pausing to find out who was calling.

But it was four o'clock and, as was the case every day, it was most likely his mother.

'That's lovely, dear! Who is this Caesar?' asked his mother.

'He is one of Grandpa's colleagues,' Arthur said with assurance. 'I hope that you'll get here by night time so

I can show you everything. Where are you?'

His mother's voice was uneasy. 'We are still in town, for the moment.'

Arthur was a bit disappointed, but today it would take more than this to wear down his victorious spirit.

'Well . . . that's okay. If you get here tonight you can see it tomorrow morning.'

His mother began speaking in her gentlest voice. 'Arthur . . . we're not going to be able to come back right away, dear.'

Arthur's small body slowly deflated, like a punctured balloon.

'There are lots of problems here,' his mother continued. 'The factory has closed and . . . Daddy has to find another job,' she admitted.

'He could come here! There's lots of work to do in the garden!' Arthur replied.

'I'm talking about a real job, Arthur. A job where he can earn some money so that all three of us can eat.'

Arthur thought about this for a few seconds. 'You know, Mum, with my system, we can grow anything we want, not just radishes. Then we would have enough for all *four* of us to eat!'

'Of course, Arthur, but people need money for more than just food. We need to pay the rent and –'

'We could all live here! There's lots of room and I'm

sure that Alfred would be happy about it. Grandma, too!'

'Listen, Arthur! Don't make things more complicated. Daddy needs a job, so we have to stay here a few more days to look for something,' she concluded gently.

Arthur didn't understand why his mother refused even to consider all his sensible solutions, but kids are used to adults not thinking logically.

'Okay,' he said.

The subject was closed, and his mother's voice was once again sweet and light.

'But just because we aren't with you doesn't mean we aren't thinking about you, especially on a day like today,' she said, 'your *b-i-r-th-day*!'

'Happy birthday, son!' his father boomed into the phone.

Arthur mumbled 'thank you' in a monotone. His father tried to sound cheerful. 'So you thought we forgot! Well, we didn't! Surprise! A tenth birthday is not easy to forget! You're a big boy now. My own big boy!'

Grandma was watching from a corner of the kitchen, as if she knew the conversation was painful for her grandson.

'Did you like your gift?' his father asked.

'He doesn't have it yet, you idiot!' his mother growled in a low voice. She tried to cover up for her husband's mistake. 'I arranged it with Grandma, Arthur, dear. Tomorrow you will go into town with her and you can choose whatever present you want.'

'Not too expensive, though!' added his father.

'Francis!' growled Arthur's mother.

'I – I was joking!' his father mumbled.

Arthur sat like a stone, holding the receiver to his ear.

'Okay, well, we'll let you go, son, because the telephone isn't free and we can't let your mother go on and on.'

Through the telephone it was possible to hear his mother smack his father on the head.

'So goodbye, son, and once more –' his parents began to sing together – 'Happy birthday to you!'

Arthur hung up, almost without emotion. It occurred to him that there was more life at the end of his bamboo pole than at the end of this telephone line.

He looked at his dog, sitting expectantly in front of him, awaiting the news.

'It wasn't the president of the water company,' said Arthur. He suddenly felt a real moment of loneliness – a hole inside that was round and dark.

Alfred offered his ball one more time, as a way of changing the subject, but a little song called their attention away from their sad thoughts.

'Happy birthday!' Grandma sang in a full, happy

voice. She appeared from the kitchen, carrying a large chocolate cake on a platter, ten proud candles on top. To the rhythm of Alfred's barking – he couldn't stand for people to sing without him – she entered the room and placed the cake in front of Arthur.

His face lit up. Grandma laid two small presents alongside the cake as she finished the song.

Arthur threw his arms around his grandmother. 'You are the most beautiful and the most fabulous grandmother ever!' he cried wholeheartedly.

'And you are the sweetest grandson ever. Go ahead, blow out the candles!'

Arthur took a deep breath, then stopped.

'It's too beautiful. Let them burn a little longer. Let's open the presents first!'

'If you want to,' Grandma relented, amused. 'That one is from Alfred.'

'It's very nice of you to have thought of me, Alfred!' said Arthur with some astonishment.

'Well, have you ever forgotten his birthday?' Grandma asked.

Arthur smiled at that and opened the little package.

It was a brand-new tennis ball! He was dumbfounded.

'Wow! We've never had a brand-new one. It's awesome!'

Alfred barked, ready to play. Arthur prepared to

throw the ball, but his grandmother intervened. 'If you could please wait until you are outside to play ball, I would really appreciate it!' she said.

Arthur nodded, and hid the ball behind his back, between two couch cushions. He opened the next package.

'And that one is from me,' Grandma said.

It was a miniature racing car with a tiny key on the side for winding up the spring that served as a motor.

'It's magnificent!' Arthur cried. He immediately wound up the little car and placed it on the floor. With a few growls to simulate the rumbling of a motor, he released the car, which shot across the living room, followed closely by Alfred.

The car ricocheted several times and finally shook off the dog by sliding under a chair and out the other side.

Arthur roared with laughter.

'I think he prefers the car to the ball!'

The car ended up against the front door, with Alfred still scrabbling under the chair looking for it.

Arthur looked at his cake again, but still did not want to blow out the candles.

'How did you make a cake? I thought the oven was broken,' Arthur asked.

'Mrs Rosenberg let me use her oven, plus a few of

her utensils. She kept the cake at her store and that's the errand I was doing while you were buying all those straws.'

'It's wonderful,' said Arthur, who could not take his eyes off it. 'It's just a little too big for only three of us,' he added sadly.

'Don't be angry at your parents, Arthur. They're doing the best they can. I am sure that as soon as your father finds a job, everything will be all right.'

'They missed my birthday other years, too. I don't think a new job is going to change anything,' Arthur said. Unfortunately, there was nothing Grandma could say or do to prove him wrong.

Arthur prepared to blow out the candles.

'First make a wish,' his grandmother suggested.

Arthur did not have to think for very long.

'I wish that on my next birthday . . . Grandpa will be here to share it with me.'

It was hard for Grandma to hold back a tear. She touched her grandson's face.

'I hope that your wish will come true, Arthur,' she said. 'Go on now, blow them out, unless you want to eat a cake covered with wax!'

As Arthur took a deep breath, Alfred found the little car, squeezed next to the front door. But a menacing shadow loomed at the window – so menacing that the dog did not dare get close enough to pick up the toy.

The shadow approached and opened the door, causing a gust of air to swoop through and blow out the candles at the very moment that Arthur was preparing to do so.

The silhouette advanced with slow, loud footsteps towards the living room. Frozen with fear, Grandma and Arthur stayed very still.

The visitor finally moved into the light. He was about fifty years old, an imposing figure with an emaciated face that was unwelcoming, both up close and from afar.

The man removed his hat and smiled a smile that seemed to hurt his face. 'Have I arrived at a good time?' he asked.

Grandma recognized him. It was the notorious Davido, owner of the no less famous Davido Corporation – Food Suppliers. This sinister man had been trying to steal Grandma's property for years. He said he wanted to use the land for his corporation, to build apartment buildings – but Arthur and Grandma knew that Davido didn't need this land. He was just being malicious because it used to belong to his family and he wanted it back, and Grandpa wasn't around any more to stop him. Luckily, so far all Davido's attempts to get the land had been thwarted. So far.

'No, Mr Davido. You have not arrived at a good time. You are arriving at the worst possible time and I would be tempted to say *as usual*,' Grandma retorted fiercely. 'Even a minimum of politeness requires that when you visit people without prior notice, the least you can do is ring the doorbell!'

'I did try to ring,' Davido defended himself, 'and I can prove it.'

He smugly held up a piece of chain. 'One day that bell is going to fall on someone's head,' he predicted. 'The next time I will blow my car horn instead. It would clearly be safer.'

'I don't see any reason why there should be a next time,' Grandma replied. 'As for today, your visit is ill timed. We are in the midst of a family gathering.'

Davido noticed the cake, with the candles all blown out.

'Oh, look at the beautiful cake! Happy birthday, my boy! So how old are you?' He quickly counted the candles. 'Eight, nine, ten! My, how time flies!' he pretended to marvel. 'I remember when he was that small, running around after his grandfather. How long ago was that?' he said, deliberately turning the knife in the wound.

'It was four years ago,' Grandma replied with dignity.

'Four years already? Why, it seems like only yesterday!' he added with barely concealed cruelty. He searched his pockets. 'If I had known it was your birthday, boy, I would have brought something, but in the meantime –' He took a candy from his pocket and offered it to Arthur. 'Here you go. Happy birthday.'

Grandma glanced at her grandson. Her thoughts were clear. Arthur took the candy as if it were a pearl.

'Oh, how lovely. You really shouldn't have. Besides, I already have some just like it!'

Davido controlled himself, although he was dying to scold this impertinent youngster.

'I also have something for you,' he said vengefully to Arthur's grandmother.

Grandma cut him off. 'Mr Davido, I don't need anything from you except the chance to spend this afternoon alone with my grandson. So whatever the purpose of your visit may be, I would ask you to please leave this house, where you are most certainly not welcome, immediately.'

Despite her polite tone of voice, Grandma left no doubt as to the content of her message.

Davido was oblivious. He had found what he was looking for in his pockets.

'Ah! Here it is!' he said, producing from his pocket a paper neatly folded in quarters. 'Since the postman only comes to your house once a week, I made a small detour in order to save you from having to wait. Some news it's better to have as quickly as possible,' he explained with false concern.

He handed the paper to Grandma, who took it and reached for her glasses.

'It's a form stating the expiration of your deed of ownership for this property due to non-payment of taxes,' he said. 'It comes directly from the governor's office.'

Grandma began to read, her expression already annoyed.

'It had to be taken care of personally,' Davido noted. 'This matter has gone on for too long.'

Arthur did not need to read the document in order to shoot the awful man a poisonous look.

Davido smiled like a snake. 'The paper terminates your deed of ownership of this property as of today, and at the same time validates *my* deed of ownership. I suppose that explains why I feel so at home here!' He chuckled evilly.

'But rest assured,' he added, 'I am not throwing you out tonight, treating you the way you treat me. I will give you time to gather your things.'

Grandma awaited the worst.

'I am giving you seventy-two hours,' Davido said. 'In the meanwhile, please . . . make yourselves at home in my house,' he concluded maliciously.

If Arthur could have thrown a dagger with a look, Davido would have been a goner.

As for Grandma, she seemed strangely calm. She methodically reread the last paragraph of the letter before saying, 'I see a bit of a problem here.'

Davido twitched, uneasy.

'Oh, really? What problem?'

'Your good friend the governor forgot just one thing in his eagerness to be of service to you.'

'What is it?' Davido asked, too casually.

'He forgot . . . to sign it.'

Grandma handed him back the paper.

Davido was speechless. Gone were the nice words, the malevolent gestures. He stood holding the paper in front of him, mouth opening and closing like a carp.

Arthur restrained himself from jumping for joy. That would give Davido too much importance.

'So you are still here, in *my* house,' Grandma continued, 'until you can prove otherwise. And since I do not possess your legendary tact, I am giving you only ten seconds to get out before I call the police.'

Davido searched for a clever parting remark, but he couldn't think of one.

Arthur picked up the phone.

'You know how to count to ten, don't you?' the boy asked him.

'You – you are going to regret your insolence! Believe me!' Davido threatened, backing out of the room.

He turned on his heels and slammed the front door behind him with such force that his predictions came true and the doorbell fell on his head. Half senseless, blinded with pain, he blundered into the wooden column, missed the step, and fell right into the gravel.

Finally he reached his car, slammed the door on his jacket, and took off in a cloud of dust.

The sky looked as if it had been painted orange. As for the sun, it seemed to be trying to roll along the hill, as it did in the marvellous engraving that Arthur caressed with the tips of his fingers. The scene was an African savannah, bathed in the light of the end of day. You could almost feel the heat.

Arthur was in his bed, the smooth headboard smelling of apples, with a large leather book on his knees. He had chosen one of his grandfather's books, as he did every night, to accompany him to the land of dreams. He was especially excited about this one because it had been hidden behind all the others and he'd never seen it before.

Grandma sat down next to him and beamed at the sight of the engraving.

'Every night we witnessed this marvellous spectacle. And it was precisely in this setting that your mother was born,' Grandma recounted as Arthur drank in her words. 'While I was giving birth in a tent your grandfather was outside painting this landscape for me.'

Arthur smiled.

'Tell me again what you were doing in Africa,' he asked.

'I was a nurse, and your grandfather was an engineer. He built bridges, tunnels, roads. That is where we met. We were both there because we wanted to help and to learn more about the marvellous people of Africa.'

Arthur carefully turned the page and moved to the next one. It was a drawing in colour of an African tribe in full official dress, loaded down with necklaces and amulets. All the people were long and thin. They looked like distant cousins of giraffes, with the same strange gracefulness.

'Who are *they*?' asked Arthur, fascinated.

'The Bogo-Matassalai,' his grandma answered. 'Your grandfather was tied to them in friendship and to their incredible history.'

That was more than enough to excite Arthur's curiosity. 'Really? What history?'

'Not tonight, Arthur. Maybe tomorrow,' said Grandma, who was already very tired.

'Come on! Please, Grandma!' Arthur pleaded.

'I still have to straighten up the kitchen,' Grandma protested. But Arthur was shrewder than her fatigue.

'Please, just five minutes . . . it's my *birthday*!' he said in a voice that could charm a cobra.

Once again, Grandma couldn't resist.

'All right. One minute, no more,' she conceded.

'No more!' swore Arthur with a grin.

Grandma made herself more comfortable, and her grandson followed suit.

'The Bogo-Matassalai were very tall. There wasn't one adult who was less than seven feet tall. Life is not easy when you are that tall, but they believed that nature made each of them that way and that somewhere there were others who would complement them – a brother that would bring you what you do not have, and vice versa.'

Arthur was captivated. Grandma felt herself carried away along with her audience.

'The Chinese call that yin and yang. The Bogo-Matassalai gave it the name "brother-nature". And for centuries, they searched for their other half, those who would finally bring them balance.'

'Did they find them?' asked Arthur immediately, too eager to leave any time for suspense in the narrative.

'After more than three hundred years of searching throughout all the nations of Africa . . . yes,' Grandma confirmed. 'They found another tribe which was viewed by many as an object of scorn. This tribe lived right next to the Bogo-Matassalai – only a few feet away, to be precise.'

'How is that possible?' marvelled Arthur.

'This tribe was called the Minimoys and had the

peculiarity of measuring . . . barely three quarters of an inch tall!'

Grandma turned the page and they found a picture of the famous miniature tribe, posing in the shade of a dandelion.

Arthur was amazed. He had never had an inkling of these wonderful stories. Grandpa had always preferred tales of engineering accomplishments. Arthur flipped from one page to the other, as if to better appreciate the difference in size.

'And – they got along well?' he asked.

'Marvellously!' Grandma assured him. 'Each helped to do the work the other could not do. If one was cutting down a tree, the other would exterminate the insects inside it. The extremely large and the extremely small were made for each other. Together, they had a unique and total vision of the world that surrounded them.'

Arthur was fascinated. He turned the page and his gaze fell on a tiny creature that made his heart do a somersault. Two large blue eyes under a rebellious red fringe stared back at him with a look that was as mischievous as a young fox, and a small smile that could melt even the hardest heart.

Arthur did not yet realize that he had fallen in love. For the moment, he only felt a glowing warmth in his stomach and an oddly perfumed breath of air entering his lungs. Grandma watched him out of the corner of her eye, delighted to be witnessing this magical moment.

Arthur cleared his throat a few times and finally managed to say a few words.

'Who – who – who is this?' he stammered.

'That is Princess Selenia, the daughter of the king of the Minimoys,' Grandma replied. 'At least, that is what your grandfather told me. He drew this just before he disappeared. He was always talking about the Minimoys, even long after we left Africa.'

'She's beautiful,' Arthur blurted out, before getting a hold of himself. 'That is, what I meant to say is – very nice – the story, I mean. It's incredible!'

'Your grandfather was an honorary member of the Bogo-Matassalai tribe. He did a great deal for them: he built wells, irrigation systems, dams. He even taught them and the Minimoys how to use mirrors to communicate with each other and to transport energy,' Grandma said proudly. 'When it came time for us to depart, in order to thank him, they gave him a bag full of rubies, each one bigger than the next.'

'Wow!' Arthur exclaimed.

'But your grandfather didn't know what to do with this treasure. He really wanted something very different,' Grandma confided. 'He wanted the secret that would make it possible for him to visit the Minimoys.'

Arthur was mesmerized. He looked first at the drawing of Princess Selenia, then at his grandma.

'And . . . they gave it to him?' he asked, as nonchalantly as possible, although he felt as if the answer could change his life.

'I never found out,' Grandma answered. 'The war had started, so I returned home to be an army nurse, while your grandfather enlisted to fight in Africa throughout the war. For six years I had no news from him,' she said. 'Your mother and I were convinced that we would never see him again. As brave as he was, there was a good chance he had died in combat.

'And then, one day, I received a letter with a photo of this house, asking us to come live here with him!'

'And then?' asked Arthur excitedly.

'Then . . . I fainted! It was a bit too much, all at once!' Grandma confessed.

Arthur burst out laughing, imagining his grandmother with all four limbs in the air, a letter clutched in her hand.

'And then what did you do?'

'I came here. And here we stayed!' she said happily.

'Grandpa was very strong, wasn't he?' Arthur asked.

Grandma stood up and closed the book. 'Yes, and I am most certainly too weak! The minute is up. Time for bed!'

She pulled down the covers so that Arthur could slide his legs in.

'I would like to find the Minimoys, too,' he added, pulling the blanket right up to his chin. 'If Grandpa returns some day, do you think he will tell me the secret?'

'If you are a good boy and you do as I say, I will ask him for you.'

Arthur hugged her.

'Thank you, Grandma. I knew I could count on you!'

'Now, go to sleep!' she said firmly.

Arthur turned around and threw himself on his pillow, pretending to be asleep already.

Grandma kissed him affectionately, picked up the book, and turned off the light, leaving Arthur to his dreams of Selenia. She quietly entered her husband's study, avoiding the squeaky floorboards, and returned the precious book to its place. Then she stood for a moment before the portrait of her husband.

She let out a sigh that seemed enormous in the quiet of the night.

'We miss you, Archibald,' she confessed. 'We really miss you very much.'

Chapter 3

The garage door was so heavy that opening it was like opening the drawbridge of a castle, and it always took Arthur a few seconds to recover.

He got down on his knees and took his racing car out of the garage. Eight hundred horsepower in only three inches! All it took was imagination, and that was something that Arthur was never lacking.

He put his finger on the car and rolled it, adding a soundtrack of growls, vrooms, and other noises worthy of a Ferrari. He also lent his voice to the two drivers that he imagined on board, and to their boss, who was guiding them from afar.

'Gentlemen, I want a complete report on our worldwide irrigation system,' he said, cupping his hands as if talking through a loudspeaker.

'Right, chief!' he replied, pretending to be the driver.

'And be careful with this new car! It is extremely powerful!' added the loudspeaker.

'Okay, chief! Don't worry,' the driver assured him as he left the parking space and drove deep into the garden grass.

Grandma pushed open the front door. She was carrying a large basket full of wet laundry to the end of the garden to hang on the clothes-line.

Arthur steered his car as it descended into the ditch and then chugged alongside the impressive irrigation system.

'Patrol car to central. Everything appears to be in order,' the driver reported.

But the patrol spoke too soon. All at once an enormous (and brand-new) tennis ball loomed out of nowhere, completely blocking the passage.

'Oh, no! Directly ahead! It's a disaster!'

'Patrol, what's happening? Report!' cried the chief, who could see nothing from his office.

'It's a landslide! No, it's not a landslide! It's a trap! It's Bigfoot!'

Alfred had just put his nose against the other side of the tennis ball and was wagging his tail as hard as he could.

'Central to patrol. Be careful of that tail; it's a dangerous weapon!' warned the loudspeaker.

'Don't worry, chief. He seems calm for the moment. We'll take advantage of that to clear the road. Send in the crane!'

Arthur's arm was immediately transformed into a mechanical crane, with all the right accompanying noises. After a few manoeuvres, Arthur's hand-claw succeeded in catching the ball.

'Ejection!' cried the driver.

Arthur's arm extended and threw the ball as far as possible.

Not surprisingly, 'Bigfoot' ran right after it.

'The road is clear and we have got rid of Bigfoot!' the driver proudly announced.

'Well done, patrol!' said the loudspeaker. 'Continue with your mission.'

Grandma, meanwhile, had continued on *her* mission as far as the second clothes-line, where she began to hang the sheets.

Far off in the distance, on the top of the hill, a small cloud of dust signalled the arrival of a car.

But it was not the day for the postman or for the milkman.

'Now what is it?' Grandma worried.

Arthur, unaware of the approaching vehicle, was still on patrol, where a new drama was taking place. Bigfoot had returned. His paws were on the side of the trench, the ball in his mouth, ready to be released.

Inside the car there was chaos.

'Oh, no! We are doomed!' cried the co-pilot.

'Never!' the pilot decreed in Arthur's most heroic voice. Arthur furiously wound the key on top of the car.

Bigfoot dropped his bomb into the trench.

'Hurry, captain,' begged the co-pilot, 'or we are all going to die!'

The ball rolled along the trench towards them. Arthur pointed the car in the direction for escape.

'Banzai!' he yelled, even though the Japanese expression was not exactly appropriate for the situation.

The car leaped forward, propelled by the wind from the ball that was hurtling towards it at crushing speed. The racing car cut neatly across its path, like a fighter plane, shooting swiftly out of harm's way. The ball rolled off into the distance, but, unfortunately, the car was now on a collision course with the side of the trench, which appeared to be an impassable wall.

'We're doooooooomed,' moaned the co-pilot.

'Hang on!' replied Arthur, the courageous driver.

The racing car arrived at the foot of the wall and shot up it, almost vertically. It flew through the air, landing on the ground in a magnificent series of spins before finally rolling to a stop.

The chain of events had been sublime, almost perfect.

Arthur was as proud as a peacock that had invented the wheel.

'Well done, captain,' said the co-pilot, exhausted.

'It was nothing, my boy!' replied Arthur with the nonchalance of an old veteran.

A giant shadow suddenly loomed over the little racing car – that of a much bigger racing car, belonging to the sinister Davido. The larger car rolled to a stop, leaving Arthur's car trapped underneath. Through the windshield, Davido looked very pleased with himself.

Bigfoot/Alfred trotted up with his toy again, but from Arthur's expression he could tell that this was not the best time for games. With a small whine, he dropped the ball, which rolled to the end of the asphalt, crossed under the real car, and came to a stop directly under Davido's foot as he stepped out of the vehicle.

The result was unexpected. Davido stepped on the ball, slipped, fell, and found his arms and legs pinwheeling in the air.

Arthur was on the ground, too, but that's because he was laughing so hard.

'Patrol to central! Bigfoot has just claimed another victim!' announced the driver.

Alfred barked and wagged his tail.

Davido scrambled up as best he could and brushed himself off. Angrily, he grabbed the ball and threw it as far as possible. A tearing sound ripped through the silence and, at the same time, through the underarm seam of his jacket.

The ball landed in the water tank, several feet off the ground.

Furious about the damage to his jacket but satisfied with his throw, Davido rubbed his hands together.

'Your turn, "central"!' he said to Arthur vengefully.

Arthur just looked at him without saying anything.

Davido spun on his heel and headed towards the end of the garden, where Grandma had just hung one of the sheets lengthwise across the clothes-line and was turning to get another from her basket.

She found herself face-to-face with Davido.

'You startled me!' Grandma scolded.

'I am so sorry,' said Davido, obviously lying. 'Spring cleaning? Do you need a hand?'

'No, thank you. What do you want now?' asked the old lady.

'I wanted to apologize. I made a mistake the other evening and I came to make amends,' he said slyly.

Once again, Davido whisked a piece of paper out of his pocket and flourished it under Grandma's nose.

'Here, it is fixed! Now the paper is properly signed.' He took a clothes-pin and hung the paper on the line.

'You didn't waste any time,' Grandma conceded, sick to her stomach.

'Oh, it was a lucky coincidence,' he said. 'I was going to church, like I do every Sunday morning, and who should I meet there but the governor!'

'You go to church on Sunday? That's funny, I've never seen you there,' Grandma replied implacably.

'I usually stay in the back, out of humility. I was surprised myself not to see you there this morning,' he answered. 'On the other hand, I did run into the mayor, who confirmed my deed of sale.'

Davido took out a new letter that he pinned to the clothes-line next to the previous one.

'I also ran into the notary, and he validated the purchase,' he said, hanging up yet another letter. 'Moreover, the banker and his charming wife have hereby transferred your debt on the property to me.' A fourth letter was pinned next to the others.

Unnoticed by the adults, Arthur had begun to climb up the north side of the water tank.

Alfred was watching from below. He did not look very happy about the situation.

Davido continued to hang up letters. He was already on the ninth.

'The surveyor, who authenticated the property lines,' he continued relentlessly. 'And, finally, the police commissioner, who countersigned the notice for your eviction within seventy-two hours.'

He proudly hung up the tenth and last letter.

'That makes ten! My lucky number!' he added with sadistic glee.

Grandma was vexed and speechless.

'There. So, unless your husband returns to do his taxes or you settle your debts within the next seventy-two hours, this house will be mine.'

'You have no heart, Mr Davido,' Grandma finally managed.

'Not true! I have a rather generous nature. That is why I have previously offered you a good sum for this miserable property! But you wouldn't hear of it!'

'The house has never been for sale, Mr Davido!' Grandma reminded him for the hundredth time.

'See what a bad attitude you have,' he replied.

Arthur balanced himself on the edge of the large tank, which was half full of water. The tennis ball floated peacefully on the surface.

Arthur imagined himself as an acrobat. He squeezed his legs around the wooden edge and reached out for the ball.

Alfred began to whine. It's funny how animals can sense an impending drama.

And in fact – there was a *crack*. A small one. Almost ridiculous, but enough to send Arthur plummeting into the tank with an enormous splash.

Alfred trotted off, his tail between his legs.

*

'Why do you want this tiny piece of land and this "miserable" house so much?' Grandma inquired acidly.

'I plan to build apartments here, as you know. And I want it for sentimental reasons. This land belonged to my parents,' the businessman replied coldly.

'I know. It was your parents who generously offered it to my husband for all of the services he had done for the region. Do you really want to violate the wishes of your late parents?' Grandma questioned.

Davido was clearly ill at ease.

'Late! That's a good word. They are *late*, just like your husband is late, and they left me all alone!' Davido said edgily.

'Your parents did not abandon you. They died during the war,' Grandma corrected.

'The result was the same!' he shouted. 'They left me alone, and so it is alone that I intend to conduct my business! And if your husband has not paid his debt by noon three days from now, I shall be obliged to evict you, whether your laundry is dry or not!'

Davido lifted his chin, turned around, and came face-to-face with Arthur, who was standing there drenched from head to foot. The businessman clucked disapprovingly, sounding rather like a turkey when it finds out that it has been invited for Christmas dinner.

'You should hang him out to dry, too!' he added in a mocking tone.

Arthur glared at him.

Davido headed off towards his car, still clucking. He slammed the door, turned on the engine, and let the wheels spin, kicking up a thick cloud of dust. The little racing car was knocked out of the car's shadow, somersaulted a few times, rolled backward a bit, and fell into the opening of a drainpipe.

Davido took off, followed by his thick cloud, which settled over all the clothes that were hung out to dry. Arthur and his grandmother were also coated with the yellow dust.

Exhausted, Grandma sat down on the front steps.

'My poor Arthur. This time I don't think I will be able to stop that greedy Davido,' she said sadly.

'Didn't he used to be a friend of Grandfather's?' Arthur asked, sitting down next to his grandmother.

'At first he was,' she admitted. 'When we arrived from Africa, Davido couldn't tear himself away from your grandfather! He stuck to him like glue. But Archibald never really trusted him, and he was right.'

'Will we have to leave the house?' asked Arthur worriedly.

'I am afraid so,' the poor woman admitted.

Arthur was overwhelmed by the news. How could he live without this garden, the place for all his games, his sole refuge? And where would his grandmother go? He had to find a solution.

'What about the treasure? The rubies offered by the Bogo-Matassalai?' he asked, full of hope. 'What did Grandpa do with all that? Couldn't we use it to save the house?'

Grandma pointed to the garden.

'It's out there, somewhere.'

'You mean – the treasure is hidden in the garden?' Arthur asked.

'That's what your grandfather told me. So well hidden that even though I have dug everywhere, I have never been able to find it,' Grandma confessed.

Arthur was already on his feet. He grabbed the little shovel leaning against the wall and ran to the middle of the garden.

'What are you doing, dear?' Grandma asked.

'Do you think I'm just going to sit back for seventy-two hours while that vulture steals our house from us?' replied Arthur. 'I am going to find that treasure!'

Arthur energetically jammed his shovel into a small patch of grass and began to dig like a bulldozer. Alfred was delighted with this new game, barking encouragement and running in circles.

Grandma could not help smiling.

'He is the spitting image of his grandfather,' she remarked. Brushing off her knees, she noticed she was covered with dust. She got up with difficulty and went back into the house to change her clothes.

A few drops of sweat had beaded on Arthur's forehead. He was already digging his third hole.

Suddenly, his shovel hit something hard. Alfred barked, as if he could sense something. Arthur got down on his knees and continued digging with his hands.

'If you've found the treasure, you really are the best dog in the world!' Arthur said to his dog, who was wagging his tail almost hard enough to take flight.

Arthur burrowed into the ground a little more, brushed his hand along the object, and pulled it out of the ground.

It was a bone.

'That's not the kind of treasure we are looking for, you wild animal! We need a real treasure!' exclaimed Arthur, throwing away the bone and starting to dig a new hole.

The door to Archibald's office opened slowly. Grandma took a few steps in and looked around at the space. A real museum, it was. She carefully took down one of the African masks and looked at it for a moment.

Her eye caught that of her husband, gazing down from his portrait.

'I am sorry, Archibald, but we no longer have a choice,' she said bitterly.

She lowered her eyes and left the room, the African mask under her arm.

Arthur reached the bottom of a new hole, where he found yet another bone. Alfred pretended to be surprised, too.

'Did you rob a butcher shop or something?' Arthur asked him in an exasperated voice.

Grandma came out of the house with the mask, which was carefully wrapped in paper so her grandson wouldn't see it.

'I – I have to do some shopping in town,' she said.

'Do you want me to go with you?' Arthur asked politely.

'No, no! Continue to dig – that's a good idea! After all, you never know.' She quickly got into the old Chevrolet and started the engine. 'I won't be long!' she cried over the noisy motor.

The pick-up took off in a cloud of dust.

Arthur was somewhat perplexed by the sudden departure of his grandmother, but duty called. He returned to digging.

Chapter 4

The pick-up came to a halt in the centre of a large city. This was nothing like the charming village where Grandma regularly did her shopping. This was a real metropolis, several miles away. Here the shops displayed their wares to hundreds of curious shoppers. Here everything seemed prettier, bigger, richer.

Grandmother held her head high, determined not to let the big city make her feel small.

She stopped in front of a shop and took a business card out of her purse. Verifying that she was at the correct address, she entered the small antique shop. At least, it appeared small from the window, but inside it seemed to go on for ever. Hundreds of objects and pieces of furniture of all kinds and from all periods were piled high. Fake Roman gods made of stone stood next to genuine Mexican saints made of wood. Fossils spilled out from porcelain vases like an invitation to a massacre. Old books bound in leather leaned next to simple paperbacks and seemed to coexist peacefully despite their differences in age and language.

Behind the counter, the owner was reading the newspaper. Part antiques dealer, part pawnbroker, nothing about the man inspired trust. As Grandma approached, wading through the junk, he did not even bother to look up.

'Can I help you?' he said automatically.

Grandma jumped at the sound of his voice. 'Excuse me,' she said, nervously showing him the business card. 'You were at our house some time ago, and you mentioned – if one day we wanted to sell some of our old furniture or objects . . .'

'Yes, that is possible,' he replied vaguely.

'Well, I have . . . an object that comes from a personal collection,' Grandma stammered. 'I would like to know if it has any value.'

The man sighed as he put down his newspaper and slipped off his glasses. He folded the paper and took the mask into his hands.

'What is this?' he asked. 'A carnival mask?'

'No. It is an African mask. This one belonged to the chief of the Bogo-Matassalai tribe. It is unique,' said Grandma with pride and respect, hiding her resentment at having to let go of such a beautiful artefact.

The antiques dealer seemed interested. He studied it for a minute.

'A dollar fifty,' he said with assurance.

Grandma gasped.

'A dollar fifty? That's impossible! This is a unique item, of inestimable value, which –'

The antiques dealer did not give her time to finish her sentence.

'Fine. A dollar eighty. That's the best I can do,' he said. 'This type of exotic item doesn't sell very well right now. People want practical items, concrete, modern. I'm sorry. Do you have anything else?'

Grandma was bewildered.

'If – perhaps . . . I don't know,' she stammered. 'What *is* selling well right now?'

The antiques dealer finally smiled.

'Without question . . . books!'

Arthur threw aside his shovel, discouraged. Alfred, on the other hand, was perfectly happy with his pile of bones. The garden now resembled a minefield.

Arthur filled a large glass of water from the kitchen tap and drank it down in one gulp. Then he went to Grandma's room, took down the key hanging on the bedpost, and headed for his grandfather's study.

He entered slowly, lit one of the beautiful Venetian lamps, and sat down at the desk.

For a long time, he stared at the portrait of his grandfather who, despite his smile, remained silent.

'I can't find it, Grandpa,' Arthur said sadly. 'I can't believe that you hid this treasure in the garden without leaving word anywhere, any sign or hint, anything that would help us to find it. It doesn't seem like you.'

The painting continued to smile. Archibald was still silent.

'Unless . . . maybe I haven't looked for it correctly?' Arthur grabbed the first book above the desk and began to leaf through it.

Several hours passed. Arthur had gone through almost all the books, piling them high on the desk. Night had finally fallen and he ached all over.

He finished with the book that his grandmother had read to him the night before. Once again he saw the drawing of the Bogo-Matassalai, then that of the Minimoys. He skipped a few pages and came across a much more disturbing drawing.

It was an evil shadow, like an emaciated body, only vaguely human-looking. The face had no expression and only two red points for eyes.

A shiver ran through Arthur from head to foot. It was by far the ugliest thing he had ever seen in his short life.

Under the drawing of the shadowy creature was handwritten: *Maltazard the Cursed*.

Outside, in the darkness, two yellow eyes were trailing their way along the hilltops. It was an ordinary van, piercing the night with its powerful headlights. Guided by the full moon, the vehicle followed the winding road that led to the house.

Arthur quickly turned the pages, trying to forget the nightmare vision of Maltazard as quickly as possible. He found the drawing of Selenia, the Minimoy princess.

This made him feel much better. He touched the drawing with the tips of his fingers and noticed that it was only loosely glued down. Carefully he slid a thumbnail underneath and detached it, so that he could contemplate the princess a little closer.

'I hope that I will have the honour of meeting you one day, princess,' he whispered to it.

Alfred sighed pointedly.

'Jealous,' Arthur said with a grin. The dog did not deign to reply.

Just then they heard a vehicle rolling up and parking outside. Arthur thought it was probably Grandma, returning at last.

He absentmindedly turned over the drawing and discovered another one on the back. The boy's face lit up.

'I *knew* he had left a sign!' he yelped joyously.

The drawing was a map – to the land of the Minimoys! It was sketched in pencil, rather poorly drawn or perhaps done very quickly.

There was also a sentence that Arthur read out loud: '"To find the country of the Minimoys, trust in Shakespeare." Who is that?' he asked himself. He stood up and turned the map in all directions. Something about the location seemed oddly familiar.

'So the entrance to the Minimoys' world is here, next to this tree . . . Wait, I know this tree! And here's the house, and that way's north . . .'

He ran over to the window and threw it open.

The map corresponded exactly to the view that he had from the study window.

'The large oak tree, the garden gnome, the moon, everything is there!' exclaimed Arthur. 'We found it, Alfred! We found it! The Minimoys are in the garden! I *know* they will be able to help us! I bet Grandpa must have told them where the treasure is!'

He leaped up and down with joy, like a kangaroo that had swallowed a spring.

He turned towards the door, eager to share his discovery with his grandmother, but instead he ran straight into the antiques dealer with his two movers.

'Careful, young man, careful!' said the antiques dealer, deftly steering him aside.

Despite his surprise, Arthur had instinctively hidden the drawing behind his back. The man went out into the corridor again to speak to Grandma.

'It is open, ma'am. Open and occupied!'

Grandma came out of her room and joined them.

'Arthur, I have told you that I do not want you playing in this room,' she said nervously. She caught Arthur by the arm and pulled him back so the antiques dealer could pass.

'Please excuse him. Go on in, please,' Grandma said politely.

The antiques dealer glanced around the study, like a vulture checking that a corpse is really dead.

'There, now *this* is interesting,' he said, with a calculating smile.

Arthur discreetly tugged his grandmother's sleeve.

'Grandma? Who are these people?' he whispered in a worried voice.

She wrung her hands. 'It's – the man is here to . . . appraise your grandfather's things. If we have to move, we might as well get rid of all this old stuff,' she said, trying to convince herself as much as him.

Arthur was dumbfounded.

'You're going to sell Grandpa's things?'

Grandma paused – a brief hesitation, a moment of remorse – then let out a long sigh. 'I am afraid that we don't have a choice, Arthur.'

'Of course we do, of course we have a choice!' cried the boy, waving his drawing. 'Look! This will help us find the treasure! Grandpa left us a message! It's all here on the map!'

Grandma didn't understand.

'Where did you get that?'

'It was under our noses all the time, in that book you read me last night!' Arthur explained.

But Grandma was too tired to listen to fantasies. 'Put that back where it belongs immediately,' she said severely.

'Grandma, you don't understand! It's a map to find the Minimoys! They are out there, somewhere in the garden. Grandpa must have brought them back from Africa with him. And if we can find them, I am sure that they will be able to guide us to Grandfather's treasure. We are saved!' he declared.

Grandma wondered how her grandson could have gone mad in such a short time.

'This is no time to play, Arthur. Put that back where it belongs and keep quiet.'

'You don't believe me. You think Grandpa was just telling stories!'

Grandma placed her hand on his shoulder. 'Arthur, you're a big boy now, aren't you? Do you really believe that the garden is full of tiny elves who are just waiting for you to visit so they can give you a bag of rubies?'

The antiques dealer whipped his head around, like a fox catching a scent.

'Excuse me?' he asked politely.

'No, nothing . . . I was speaking to my grandson,' Grandma answered.

The antiques dealer continued his inspection as if nothing had happened, but his ears were alert. 'Of course, if you also have jewellery, we buy that as well,' he said, the way you would toss bread out to pigeons.

'Unfortunately, there are no jewels on the horizon!' Grandma answered firmly. Once again she turned towards Arthur. 'Now put that drawing back where it belongs, and fast!'

The boy obeyed reluctantly, while the antiques dealer read the banner hanging above the desk like a birthday garland:

'"Words often hide other words. William S."' The antiques dealer seemed amused by this enigmatic sentence. '*S* – for Socrates?' he asked.

'No, *S* for Shakespeare. William Shakespeare,' Grandma said.

This rang a bell in Arthur's head and he slid out the drawing again. He reread the phrase on the back: *To find the country of the Minimoys, trust in Shakespeare.*

'Ah? . . . Well, I was close,' exclaimed the antiques dealer.

Grandma threw him a sharp look. 'Yes. Only two thousand years out of the neighbourhood.'

‘How quickly time flies!’ he said, trying to hide his ignorance.

‘You are right, time does fly, so please hurry up and make your selection before I change my mind,’ Grandma answered.

‘We’ll take everything!’ The antiques dealer gestured to his men.

Grandmother was speechless. Arthur started to slide the drawing into the back pocket of his trousers, but he wasn’t quick enough.

‘Tsk, tsk! No cheating, my boy!’ said the antiques dealer with an inquisitor’s smile. ‘I said we will take . . . everything!’

Regretfully, Arthur took the paper out of his pocket and handed it to the antiques dealer, who quickly placed it in his jacket pocket.

‘That’s right, my boy,’ said the dealer slyly, patting him on the head.

The movers began their work. Furniture and objects disappeared with frightening speed, under the tearful eyes of the poor woman who was watching years of memories slip away. The scene was as sad as a forest going up in smoke.

One of the movers grabbed the portrait of Archibald. Grandma stopped him as he passed, seizing the edge of the frame.

‘No. Not that,’ she said firmly.

'He said everything!' the mover protested.

Grandma began to yell. 'And I say everything *except* the portrait of my husband!'

The employee looked at his boss, who decided this might not be worth the trouble.

'Simon! Leave her husband alone! He didn't do anything to you!' joked the antiques dealer. He took the painting and held it out to the old lady.

'Here. Take it, ma'am. A gift on the house!' he had the nerve to add.

The back door of the van was opened and the two movers piled in the last boxes. Arthur lay stretched out on the living room couch, watching his grandmother at the doorway as she finished her negotiations with the antiques dealer.

The man counted out the bills and put the pile in her hand.

'There you go. Three hundred dollars in cash!' he announced proudly.

'That's a small sum of money for thirty years of memories,' Grandma murmured.

'It's an advance,' the merchant assured her. 'If I sell everything, you will have an additional sum of at least ten per cent per item!'

'Marvellous!' Grandma replied ironically.

'The antiques fair takes place in ten days. If you change your mind, you can always come and get them before then,' advised the antiques dealer.

'That is very kind of you,' she replied dryly.

She opened the front door to escort the antiques dealer out, and found herself face-to-face with a short man in a grey suit, accompanied by two policemen. There was no need for a detective to identify the short man as a sheriff.

'Mrs Suchot?' the lawman asked politely, although the tone of his voice left no doubt as to the purpose of his visit.

'Yes,' Grandma replied.

One of the two police officers tried to reassure her with a small, friendly wave and she realized it was Martin, her friend from outside the supermarket. The man in grey continued.

'I am Frederick Sinclair. The sheriff.'

The antiques dealer could tell it was time for a quick exit.

'See you soon, ma'am. It was a pleasure doing business with you!' he said, taking off into the night.

The pile of bills that Grandma was holding in her hand caught the sheriff's eye.

'I see I came at just the right time!' he said. He pulled out a letter. 'I have a notice against you demanding payment for work done on your house several years ago by one Ernest Davido. It amounts to a sum of one hundred and eighty-five dollars, to which has been added a late penalty of six per cent along with the court costs. That comes to a total of two hundred and ninety dollars.'

Grandma looked at her pile of banknotes and handed them over, dazed.

The sheriff grabbed them, somewhat surprised at not having to fight for them.

'May I?' he said, counting the bills with lightning speed.

Arthur watched this scene from the couch. He was neither disturbed nor astonished, simply disgusted. He understood that his grandmother had been thrust into a downward spiral from which she could not escape.

'Unless I am mistaken . . . three dollars are missing,' said the sheriff.

'I don't understand – I – that should be exactly three hundred dollars!' Grandma replied with astonishment.

'Do you want to count them yourself?' he asked, with great politeness and no doubt. There was little chance that he had made a mistake. He was like an undertaker's assistant – if he tells you that his client is dead, you can count on it.

Grandma was overwhelmed. She slowly shook her head.

'No, you must be right.'

In his van travelling through the night, the antiques dealer rubbed his hands together with satisfaction.

'That was a nice little deal. Well handled,' he confided to his assistant, laughing. He dug his hand into his pocket. 'Now let's see what that little monster was trying to hide from us.'

He took out the paper that Arthur had given him so reluctantly and unfolded it slowly with pleasure.

It was a supermarket shopping list.

Chapter 5

In the living room, it was Arthur's turn to unfold his paper – the drawing of Princess Selenia that he had subtly exchanged. He studied the drawing as if it were his only hope.

The sheriff continued with his business. 'In spite of the small sum still due, I'm afraid the law is the law. I am going to have to seize property in order to recover the missing three dollars,' he announced.

Martin, the nice officer, felt obliged to intervene. 'Wait!' He took out his wallet. 'There . . . three dollars. Now the account is clear!' he said, handing over the money.

The sheriff shifted awkwardly.

'That's – well, this is very irregular, but . . . given the circumstances, I accept!'

Grandma was on the verge of tears, but she managed

to keep her dignity.

'Thank you, officer. I – I will repay you as soon as . . . as soon as I can!'

'Don't worry about it, Mrs S. I am sure that as soon as your husband returns, together you will find a way to pay me back,' he said kindly.

'I'll see to it,' Grandma replied.

The policeman grabbed the sheriff by the shoulder and pulled him away.

'You've done enough work for today, sir. We're leaving now.'

The sheriff did not dare contradict him.

'Ma'am, my respects,' he said as they walked away.

Grandma closed the door and leaned against it for a moment, stunned.

The telephone next to Arthur rang. He picked up the receiver.

'Hello? Arthur, dear? It's Mum! How are you?' whistled the voice in the receiver.

'Great! Things are great,' Arthur replied sarcastically. 'Grandma and me, we're just great!'

Grandma came into the living room and made signs to her grandson that clearly meant: Don't tell them anything.

'What have you been up to?' his mother asked, not really paying attention.

'Straightening up!' said Arthur. 'It's amazing how

many useless old things one can find in a house. But, thanks to Grandma, we've thrown everything out!'

'Arthur, please, don't upset them!' Grandma whispered.

Arthur hung up the phone.

'Arthur! Did you just hang up on your mother?' Grandma asked, shocked.

'Of course not. The line disconnected,' he explained, heading for the stairs.

'So where are you going? Stay here – she'll probably call you back in a minute.'

Arthur stopped in the middle of the stairs and looked hard at his grandmother.

'They cut off the phone service, Grandma! Don't you see what is happening? You are caught in a trap. A trap that every hour is getting tighter and tighter. But I'm not going to let them do it. As long as I live, they will not have this house!'

Arthur had probably heard this expression in an adventure film, but he said it very well. He turned around and proudly climbed the stairs.

Grandma picked up the phone and saw that he was right – the line had gone dead.

'It's probably temporary. That happens sometimes when there's a storm,' she said.

'It hasn't rained for more than a month,' Arthur called down from the top of the stairs.

The doorbell rang.

'You see? That must be the repair man,' Grandma reassured herself. She hurried to the door, where, indeed, and much to her surprise, a workman in uniform was waiting.

'Evening, ma'am!' said the workman, tipping the brim of his hard hat.

'Oh, you are just in time!' said Grandma. 'The telephone cut off just a moment ago. I think that the least they can do is warn people about something like that, don't you?'

'I agree with you, ma'am,' the technician politely conceded. 'But I'm not here about the telephone. I'm from the electricity company.' He pointed to the badge sewn on his jacket as proof. 'I have come to warn you that your electricity will be turned off soon because of lack of payment.'

He pulled out an official form and handed it to her.

Arthur entered the empty study. Besides a few worthless objects, there remained only the desk, a chair, the banner, and the portrait of Grandfather.

He flopped angrily down in the chair and looked at the banner, thinking it was miraculous that it had been left behind. Clearly the bit of cloth was of very little value, even if the advice that it gave was priceless.

'"Words often hide other words,"' Arthur reread out loud.

The puzzle was right there in front of him. He was sure of it.

'Help me, Grandfather. If words often hide other words, what is the secret that these words are hiding?'

The painting remained silent.

Grandma finished reading the blue form and gave it back to the workman.

'And . . . when will the electricity be turned off?' she asked.

'Very soon, I think!' the workman answered. At the exact moment the lights blinked out through the entire house.

'That *was* quick,' Grandma said. 'Don't move. I'll go find a candle.'

Upstairs, Arthur lit a match and brought it up to light a candle. He placed the candle on the desk and stepped back a few feet, in order to better see the banner, the key to the riddle.

'Now is the time to be brilliant!' he challenged himself. '"Words . . . often . . . hide . . . other . . . words."'

The candlelight accented the transparency of the banner and Arthur suddenly thought he caught a glimpse of something.

He took the candle in his hand, climbed up on the chair, and placed the light just behind the banner. Lit from behind, words appeared. Words hiding behind other words! Arthur grinned.

'Of course!' he exclaimed.

He ran the candle behind the banner and read the hidden message as best he could. He could almost hear the deep, hoarse voice of his grandfather, as if he were there in the room.

My dear Arthur, I was sure I could count on you and that you would see through this simple charade.

Arthur grimaced. 'Not so simple,' he answered his grandfather.

The voice continued.

You must be close to ten years old now to be so smart. On the other hand, I'm not so smart, because if you are reading these lines, I am probably dead.

Arthur stopped for a moment, a chill running through him. Imagine his grandfather, once so alive, already dead! He could not even bring himself to think about it.

The difficult task of finishing my mission is up to you. If you agree, of course.

Arthur looked up at his grandfather's portrait. The confidence that the old man had had in him made his chest swell with pride. 'I do agree, Grandfather,' he said solemnly, before turning back to the message.

I expected nothing less of you, Arthur. You are worthy of being my grandson, Grandpa had written.

Arthur smiled, astonished by the old man's clairvoyance.

'Thank you,' he answered.

The writing continued: *To find the land of the Minimoys, you must first know on what date the next passage will take place. There is only one opportunity each year. You must take the universal calendar that is on my desk and count the seventh moon of the year. On the night of the seventh moon, precisely at midnight, the light will open the door to the land of the Minimoys.*

Arthur couldn't believe it. Everything that he had imagined was true.

The hidden treasure, the Minimoys, and . . . Princess Selenia.

He let out a small, happy sigh, then took hold of himself and bent towards the desk to find the calendar. Fortunately, the antiques dealer had left it behind. Arthur quickly consulted it and counted the full moons.

'Four . . . five . . . six . . . seven!'

He looked at the corresponding date.

'July thirty-first. The day after my birthday! That's – that's *tonight*!' he realized with alarm.

Arthur turned towards the clock hanging on the wall. It read 10.56 p.m.

'That's in one hour!' he cried, panic-stricken.

*

Grandma, by candlelight, finished signing the paper that the technician had amiably handed her.

'There. The pink copy is for you, the blue is for me. One for the girls, one for the boys,' he tried to joke, but the humour fell flat. Grandma remained as hard as a piece of marble. He continued hurriedly, 'To have the electricity reconnected, just go to the main office, weekdays between nine a.m. and six p.m. – with a cheque, obviously.'

'Obviously,' echoed Grandma, before adding with curiosity: 'Tell me, why are you still working at this late hour? It's nearly midnight, isn't it?'

'Believe me, I'm not happy about it, but the head office made me,' confided the employee. 'They absolutely insisted that I come here this evening. They even paid me triple overtime! You'd think there was someone here that D.G.E. doesn't like!'

'D.G.E.?' Grandma inquired.

'Davido General Electric,' the technician explained.

'Ah! I understand now!' Grandma sighed.

Suddenly an odd noise was heard coming from upstairs. It sounded like hammer blows.

The technician uneasily tried another joke.

'Looks like I'm not the only one working overtime tonight!'

'No. Those are our ghosts,' said Grandma with assurance. 'The house is full of them. You should probably leave as soon as possible, because they really can't stand uniforms.'

The technician looked at himself from head to toe. No one was more in uniform than him. He smiled weakly, but, just in case, opted to leave.

'That's fine! Okay, I'll leave you alone now!' he said, backing into the garden. As soon as he reached the limit of the candle's light, he turned and ran to his car.

Grandma smiled, closed the door, and tilted her head to determine from where those hammering sounds were coming from.

Chapter 6

Arthur was madly banging on a section of the study wall (with the help of a hammer, of course). He hoped he'd understood the next part of his grandfather's message correctly. This looked like the plank he'd said to hammer on thirty times, but Arthur was not sure what was supposed to happen after all this pounding.

'Twenty-eight . . . twenty-nine . . . and thirty!' he breathed.

The last blow was harder than the others and it made the small plank pop out of the wall. Arthur could see now that the piece of wood was mounted on a pivot. It was the door to a tiny hiding place.

Arthur slipped his hand into the small space and pulled out a piece of paper. He unfolded it and quickly read:

Bravo. You have solved the second riddle. Here is the third and last. Go to the old radiator. Turn the valve towards the right, as many turns as there are letters in your first name. Then turn it back a quarter of a turn.

Arthur squeezed under the window and knelt in front of the old radiator. He grabbed the valve and began to turn it.

'Arthur! A . . . R . . . T . . . H . . . U . . . R!' He had no time to waste. 'And now I just have to turn it one quarter to the left.' He paused and took a deep breath, as if preparing himself for the worst.

The worst arrived at the door. Grandma burst in and Arthur jumped.

'*Now* what are you doing? What was that hammering sound?' she asked, exhausted by this endless nightmare of a day.

'I – I am fixing Grandfather's radiator!' Arthur stammered. He wondered if he should show her the messages. But she didn't believe him before – what if she didn't believe him now? And wouldn't she be proud if he found the treasure all by himself? He decided he should probably keep it all a secret for now.

'The radiator? In the middle of the night? And in the middle of the summer?' asked Grandma, not really fooled by his lie.

'You never know. Sometimes winter arrives without warning. You're the one who says that all the time!' Arthur replied sensibly.

'It's true, I do say that. But usually in November!' she pointed out. 'I also say that it's almost midnight and therefore time for you to go to bed. And I've also told you a hundred times that I don't want you in this room!'

'Why? There's nothing left in it now,' Arthur replied sadly.

Grandma realized that she no longer had any real justification, but she insisted, on principle.

'True, there are no more objects – but the memories are always here and I don't want you to disturb them!' she concluded. She walked over to the calendar on the wall and tore off the page for 31 July, revealing the page for 1 August. The torn-off page went into a small box which was labelled THE DAYS WITHOUT YOU in black marker. The pile was rather large.

'Go on! Off to bed!'

Arthur obeyed reluctantly, while Grandma locked the study door with the key, which she put back in its place on the post of her bed. She joined her grandson in his room as he finished putting on his pyjamas.

Grandma turned down his covers. The boy slid in without saying a word.

'A short story, but no more than five minutes,' said Grandma gently, trying to make amends.

'No, thanks. I'm tired,' Arthur replied, closing his eyes.

Grandma was a little surprised, but did not argue. She smoothed down his hair, took the candle, and went out the door, leaving the room bathed in moonlight.

As soon as the door was shut, the boy jumped up and stretched.

'You can do it, Arthur!' he said to give himself some courage. He half opened the door and listened. He could hear the noise of the shower. Grandma was taking advantage of the last few gallons of hot water.

He slipped inside her bedroom. Steam was escaping through the partially opened bathroom door. Arthur entered quietly, using his toe to test all of the floorboards that were likely to squeak.

He arrived at the bed and reached out his arm to get the key.

Prize in hand, his eyes fixed firmly on the bathroom, he crept backward to the door.

Suddenly, he bumped into something and let out a yelp of surprise. The something was in fact some*one*: his grandma – same family as her sly grandson, only with fifty more years of experience.

'You startled me!' Arthur cried. 'I – I thought you were taking a shower.'

'No, I was in the living room looking for my sleeping drops,' she said, holding up the little bottle of herbal medicine. 'And I advise you to go back to bed as fast as you can if you don't want me to make you drink the entire bottle!'

She pulled the key out of Arthur's hands, and he went dejectedly back to his room. Grandma sighed, replaced the key on its nail, and followed him. By candlelight, she discovered the boy in bed with the sheets pulled up to his chin.

'You have to sleep now, Arthur.'

'I know,' said Arthur, panicked by the fact that time was passing and there wasn't anything he could do.

'I'll close your door with a key. That will help you to avoid any temptation,' Grandma said kindly.

Up close, one could hear Arthur gulp with alarm. But Grandma was too far away to hear. She smiled at him, went out, and locked the door behind her.

Arthur pulled off the covers and got up right away. His sheets and his covers were already attached to one another. All he had to do was open the window and throw them out.

He climbed onto the window ledge and slid down his makeshift ladder to the ground.

Grandma placed the candle on the little night table next to her bed. The weak light still made it possible to read the time on the old alarm clock.

It was twenty-five minutes to twelve.

The little flame also helped her count her drops:

three exactly, at the bottom of a large glass of water, which she drank in a single gulp. She then refilled the glass with water in case she needed it during the night.

She blew out the candle, placed her glasses on the little table and stretched out, letting sleep overtake her.

Arthur let himself drop from his cloth rope, which was too short to reach the ground. He got to his feet and ran as fast as he could to the front door.

Alfred jumped up when he saw Arthur arrive. He, who guarded the front door so proudly, was astonished to see Arthur outside. How had his master got past him?

Since the front door was locked, Arthur had to wriggle through the little flap door meant for the dog. For Alfred, it was one surprise after another. There was his master, walking on all fours and using *his* door!

Almost by reflex, Arthur slid in his socks across the living room floor. The large clock was ticking and indicated the time: twenty minutes to twelve.

Climbing the stairs was easy enough but he ran into problems at his grandmother's bedroom door: she had locked it.

'Oh, no!' Arthur had only a few minutes left to think.

He peered through the keyhole to be sure that the

study key was still hanging on the bedpost. It was – the only bit of good news.

'Think of something, Arthur, think of something!' he said to himself.

He stepped back, turned around, and examined everything around him very carefully, searching for a plan to grab on to. In the window above the bedroom door, he noticed that one of the panes was broken.

Arthur had an idea.

He ran down to the garage, weaving his way inside by the beam from his flashlight. He climbed on the workbench and took down one of the fishing poles carefully arranged along the wall.

Alfred jumped up once more at the sight of his master passing by with a fishing pole in his hands. The dog gave him a look that clearly said *who on earth goes fishing at this time of night?*

Arthur found a magnet on the door of one of the kitchen cabinets. He carefully slid his small, multi-purpose Swiss army knife behind the magnet and lifted it up, then attached it to the end of his fishing pole.

Without a sound, but working as quickly as possible, Arthur piled the chairs on the end table in the hall until they were high enough for him to reach Grandma's window with its broken corner. He climbed very cautiously up his makeshift scaffold and slipped the fishing pole through the small hole.

The dog watched him uncomprehendingly. There were fish in Grandma's bedroom?

Arthur carefully stretched out his pole, then lowered the line with the magnet towards the key on the bedpost.

Alfred had to investigate. He got up and trotted towards the piled-up chairs, causing one of the floorboards to creak.

Startled, Arthur was thrown off balance. He clung to the window ledge, wobbling precariously. The magnet swung back and forth in the room, knocking over the small vial on the night table, which began to drip into Grandma's glass of water.

'Arthur?' Grandma said, sitting up, half asleep.

Arthur stood still, not moving even an eyelash, and prayed that Alfred would do the same.

The dog obligingly froze, except for a very slight wag of his tail.

Grandma listened to the silence. A few crickets, one or two frogs in the garden. Nothing alarming, but this silence was too good to be true.

She reached for her glasses, not noticing the herbal sleeping drops dripping into her water. She opened her bedroom door and looked to the left, towards the stairs and Arthur's room. All she could see was the dog, sitting alone in the middle of the hall, with his tail wagging, as always.

What she didn't see was Arthur, directly behind her, high up on the chairs, his fishing pole in his hand.

'It is time for you to go to bed, too!' Grandma ordered Alfred.

Alfred slipped down the stairs, his tail between his legs. This was an order he understood.

'Why is it that nobody wants to go to sleep tonight? Is it the full moon or something?' she muttered, going back in and closing the door.

Arthur could finally breathe. It was a miracle that he had not been discovered.

Grandma took off her glasses and placed them on the night table. She took the glass of water, into which the bottle of herbal sleeping drops had emptied itself, and drank it down in one gulp, making a face.

The effect was instantaneous. Grandma fell back on the bed asleep, without even having time to turn down the covers.

Arthur continued his precarious fishing expedition, while Grandma began to snore. The magnet slowly descended towards the key and attracted it. But the bedpost seemed to disagree, clinging to its prize. Arthur frowned and yanked on the line.

The dog quietly climbed up the stairs again, wanting to know how the fishing expedition was progressing. He advanced towards Arthur, who was struggling on top of his makeshift scaffold.

Alfred stepped again on the same creaking floorboard. The foot of the end table shifted. The pile of chairs lost its fragile balance.

'Oh, NO!' Arthur yelled.

Everything collapsed like a house of cards, making an awful din. The dog took off down the stairs at high speed, barking loudly.

Arthur's head poked through the middle of a chair. The gust caused by the catastrophe had been so violent that the bedroom door swung open. Grandma had forgotten to relock it!

Arthur disentangled himself and, peering into the room, realized that his grandmother was still stretched out on her bed, snoring contentedly.

'How could she possibly have slept through all that noise?' he wondered.

He entered the bedroom, walked towards the bed, and reassured himself that his Grandma was all right. *She must be alive if she's snoring like that,* he thought. Then he noticed the overturned bottle and understood what had happened.

He took the blanket and tucked in his dear grandma, whose face looked thirty years younger thanks to the sleep she was finally getting.

'Sweet dreams, Grandmother!' he said, before picking up the key off the floor and disappearing out the door.

Chapter 7

Finally in the study, Arthur lit the candle again and turned back to the old radiator.

'One quarter turn . . . to the left,' he remembered.

He grabbed the tap and turned it. A noisy mechanism rumbled in the wall, detaching the radiator and pushing it to the side. Another hiding place was revealed, much larger than the previous one – big enough to contain a large leather trunk.

Arthur pulled the dusty trunk into the middle of the room. Inside was a magnificent copper telescope in a beautiful red velvet case. Also included was its large wooden tripod.

Arranged above the telescope in little compartments were five small African statues, all lined up next to each other. Five men in ceremonial dress – five Bogo-Matassalai.

Arthur looked at his treasure with amazement. He didn't know where to begin.

The first thing he picked up was a small key, to which was attached a label that read: ALWAYS KEEP THIS KEY WITH YOU.

Arthur placed it securely in his pocket. Then he unfolded a parchment tucked into the side of the trunk, which turned out to contain instructions and another map, rather simply laid out around the large oak in the garden.

Apparently the garden gnome covered a hole, in which the telescope had to be inserted, upside down. Then, a rug with five points (also in the trunk) had to be unfolded, and a statuette placed on each of the points.

All of this seemed simple enough. Arthur quickly memorized the directions, then took the telescope and its tripod in his arms and left the room.

As he was crossing the living room, the clock read eleven minutes to midnight.

Only eleven minutes until the opening of the door of light.

Despite the beautiful full moon, Arthur realized he could not see very much outside, especially in the shadow of the great oak tree. 'We need some light,' he said to Alfred, who was following him everywhere.

Arthur put down the telescope and headed straight for the old Chevy. He climbed in behind the steering wheel, took the keys from their hiding place under the sun visor, and tried to remember how it worked.

'Why are you looking at me like that?' he asked the dog. 'I've seen Grandma do this hundreds of times! How hard can it be?'

He turned the key in the ignition. The engine spat and coughed and spat again, unaccustomed to being awakened in the middle of the night. Arthur turned on the headlights, but the truck was not in a good position to light up the old oak tree. He would have to move it. Arthur shifted into first gear and nervously stepped on the gas, but nothing happened.

'Oh – the emergency brake, silly!' he realized.

He pulled on the handle as hard as he could and released the brake. The truck took off with a jolt. Arthur yelled and tried his best to control it as it wove and bumped around the house. The steering wheel was absolutely enormous in his hands, plus he could barely see over the dashboard. He tried his best to avoid the trees but ended up swerving into the clothes-line, and pulling down the line with all its contents.

Imagine the scene: two luminous eyes under pale white sheets, charging across the lawn, shrieking with the voice of a child. It was the perfect ghost. Is it any wonder that Alfred ran off howling? And yet, despite all the racket and the headlights sweeping the countryside, Grandma continued to sleep soundly.

The pick-up ended up rolling into the tree and lurching to a halt, but it was a very old tree and could take a few bumps. The good news was that now the light from the headlights was shining directly on the garden gnome.

Arthur hurried towards the little plaster figure and uprooted it from the ground.

'Sorry, old man,' he said as he put the gnome to one side.

The gnome had done his job well. The hole he had been hiding, which was not very wide around, seemed to go down into the earth for ever. Arthur put down the tripod and placed the large end of the telescope into the hole, as indicated on the map.

He was still perplexed as to how this strange series of actions could open a door, but he was determined to see it through.

'You stay here and keep watch. I'm going to get the rest of the stuff,' he said to his dog. Alfred gave the contraption a puzzled look as his master ran back to the house.

Arthur wrestled the heavy five-pointed rug out of the bottom of the trunk and threw it over his shoulder to drag it down the hallway. Then he slipped it through the guardrail on the stairs and picked it up in the living room.

The clock ticked steadily onward: four minutes to twelve. Arthur quickly dragged the rug outside and unfolded it so the five points were spread around the telescope, which poked through the hole in the centre. He thought it must be a wonderful sight from above, this gigantic multicoloured star spread out over the grass.

'Now the statues,' said Arthur, returning to the house once more. He removed the five African figures from the trunk with great care and headed towards the stairs.

He descended slowly, one step at a time. *I had better not break any of them, because I bet they're at the heart of the spell*, Arthur thought.

The dog had remained outside, now used to the ghost, whose yellow eyes were beginning to fade as the vehicle ran out of petrol.

But all of a sudden, shadows began to form on the ground.

Alfred pricked up his ears and shivered. The shadows slipped into the yellow light of the headlights. Enormous silhouettes . . . *worse* than ghosts.

Howling, the dog ran back to the house and shot through his small door. He tore through the living room and crashed headlong into Arthur, whose arms were filled with statuettes.

'No!' cried Arthur, but he could not stop himself from falling. The statuettes somersaulted for a moment in the air, almost in slow motion, before hurtling to the ground and smashing into a thousand pieces.

Arthur was desperate. The sight of the statues broken on the ground was unbearable.

The clock said one minute to midnight.

'I was so close. It's not fair!' he cried, his disappointment overwhelming him. He didn't even have the heart to yell at his dog, who was now hiding under the stairs.

He suddenly noticed a shadow moving across the grass outside. Arthur lifted his head and saw five enormous silhouettes bending their heads to come in the front door.

Arthur's jaw dropped open. He fumbled his small flashlight on and turned it in their direction.

The small light shone on a Bogo-Matassalai warrior in traditional dress. He wore a carefully tied tunic, decorated all over with jewels and charms. His hair was sprinkled with seashells, and he held a spear in one hand.

The man was sublime, towering – at least eight feet tall. His four colleagues were all as tall as he was.

Arthur was speechless. He felt even smaller than the garden gnome.

The warrior took a piece of paper from his pocket, unfolded it carefully, and read from it.

'Arthur?' the Bogo-Matassalai asked.

Still speechless, Arthur nodded his head. The chief smiled at him.

'There's not a moment to spare. Come!' the warrior

said to him before turning around and heading out towards the garden.

Arthur, as if hypnotized, forgot his fears and followed him. The dog followed close behind, too terrified to remain alone under the stairs.

The five Africans assumed positions at the end of each point of the cloth – taking the places of the statuettes. Arthur stood in the centre, near the telescope.

'Are you coming with me to the land of the Minimoys?' he asked nervously.

'Only one person can pass, and you are the one who must fight against M. the cursed,' the chief replied.

'Maltazard?' asked the boy, remembering the drawing in the book.

The five warriors placed their fingers on their lips, shushing him.

'Once you are on the other side, never, never, *never* say his name. It is very bad luck.'

'All right. No problem. Just M. the cursed!' Arthur repeated to himself, becoming more and more anxious.

'That is who your grandfather went to fight against. It is you who will have the honour of completing his battle,' the warrior said solemnly.

Arthur gulped. The mission sounded impossible. If his grandfather had failed . . . how could he possibly succeed?

'Thank you for the honour but – perhaps it would be better if I gave my place to one of you. You are much stronger than I am!' he said humbly.

'Your strength is from within, Arthur. Your heart is your most powerful weapon,' the warrior replied.

'Oh?' Arthur said, unconvinced. 'Perhaps, but . . . I am so small.'

The Bogo-Matassalai chief smiled at him.

'Very soon you will be a hundred times smaller still, and your strength will only become more visible.'

The clock chimed midnight.

'It is time, Arthur,' the warrior said, handing him the instructions parchment.

Arthur read it with a trembling hand, as the clock continued to strike. There were three rings around the telescope. Arthur grabbed the first.

'"The first circle, that of the body, turn three notches to the right,"' he read, trying to quell his uncertainty. He executed the move apprehensively.

Nothing happened, except that the clock chimed for the fourth time.

Arthur grabbed the second ring.

'"The second circle, that of the mind – three notches to the left!"'

He turned the second ring, which was harder to turn than the first.

The clock chimed for the eighth time. The African

chief looked up at the moon and frowned at a small cloud that was rapidly approaching.

'Hurry, Arthur!' the warrior warned in a low voice.

Arthur seized hold of the third and last ring.

'"The third circle, that of the spirit . . . one complete turn."'

Arthur breathed a deep breath and turned the ring as the clock was chiming for the eleventh time.

Unfortunately, the small cloud had reached its target, and little by little was covering the moon. The silvery light was disappearing. Arthur finished the turn and clicked the third ring into place just as the twelfth stroke of midnight pierced the silence.

Nothing happened. The Bogo-Matassalai were silent and immobile. Even the wind seemed to be holding its breath.

Arthur, worried, looked at the warriors, who were all staring up at the moon, now hidden by this little grey cloud that was unaware of the misfortune it had caused.

But all at once the wind came to their assistance and pushed away the cloud. The light from the moon began to grow stronger and stronger, and then, all of a sudden, a powerful ray blazed through the night, like a bolt of lightning linking the moon to the telescope. It lasted only a few seconds, but the shock was so great that Arthur was knocked to the ground.

Silence returned. Nothing seemed to have changed, except for the smiles on the faces of the warriors.

'The door of light is open!' the chief proudly announced. 'You may now introduce yourself.'

Arthur got up as best he could.

'Introduce myself?'

'Yes. And try to be convincing. The door remains open for only ten minutes!' the warrior added.

Arthur was immensely confused. He approached the telescope and looked through it. Of course, he couldn't see much – just a large, fuzzy brown mass.

Arthur grabbed the front of the telescope and turned it to sharpen the focus. Now he saw an opening in the ground, barely lit. The image quickly clarified until Arthur could see even the smallest bit of root.

All of a sudden, the top of a ladder appeared at the other end of the telescope.

Arthur could not believe his eyes. He looked away from the eyepiece and peered into the hole. No, he hadn't imagined it. There really was a ladder at the end of his telescope, a ladder that could not have been more than a few inches long.

He looked through the telescope once more. The ladder trembled a little, as if someone were climbing it.

Arthur held his breath. A small boy appeared at the end of the ladder and put his hands on the enormous telescope. It was a Minimoy!

Arthur was in a state of shock. Even in his wildest dreams, he would not have believed this possible.

The Minimoy cupped his hands as if he were trying to see something through the glass.

He had pointed ears, two eyes like black marbles, and freckles all over his face.

In a word, he was amazing.

Chapter 8

The Minimoy could finally make something out, although from his point of view it was simply an enormous eye.

'Archibald?' asked the little fellow with a slight gasp.

Arthur couldn't believe it. This creature spoke his language!

'Uh . . . no,' he replied, dumbfounded.

'Introduce yourself!' the Bogo-Matassalai warrior reminded him. Arthur recovered his wits and remembered his mission.

'I – I'm Archibald's grandson. I must look a bit like him. My name is Arthur.'

'I hope that you have a good reason for using the moon ray like that,' warned the Minimoy. 'The council strictly forbids its use, except in the case of an emergency.'

'It is a very great emergency,' the boy replied in as strong a voice as he could muster. 'This garden is going to be destroyed, razed to the ground, wiped out! In less than three days, there will be no more garden, no more house, and, therefore . . . no more Minimoys.'

'What are you saying? Are you a big joker, like your grandfather?' the Minimoy asked hopefully.

'This is no joke. There is a man who wants to bulldoze the land and build apartment houses!' Arthur explained to him.

'Apartment houses?!' the Minimoy repeated, horrified. 'What are apartment houses?'

'Large concrete buildings that will cover the whole garden,' Arthur replied.

'But that's horrible!' cried the Minimoy, looking terror stricken.

'Yes, it is!' Arthur agreed. 'And the only way to avoid it is if I can find the treasure that my grandfather hid in the garden. Then I can pay the man and none of this will happen.'

Betameche nodded vigorously.

'Great! Perfect! That's a very good idea!' the Minimoy said.

'But in order to find the treasure, I have to pass into your world! I need your help,' Arthur specified, as the Minimoy did not seem to have made the connection.

'Oh! But that's impossible!' replied the little creature. 'You can't just pass through like that! First we have to call a meeting of the council, and then it is necessary to explain the problem to them, and after they have deliberated maybe –'

Arthur cut him off. 'We do not have time. This door is only open for ten minutes, and then it will close for another year. By then you will all be dead!'

The Minimoy froze. He had finally understood the importance of the situation.

Arthur glanced at the African chief to be sure that he had not been too harsh. The chief raised his thumb, a sign that he had done the right thing.

'What is your name?' Arthur asked, looking back through the telescope.

'Betameche,' the Minimoy answered. 'But you can call me Beta.'

Arthur assumed a solemn voice. 'Betameche, the future of your people is in your hands.'

The Minimoy began to squirm, terrified by so much responsibility.

'Yes, of course. In my hands. We must act,' he repeated to himself in a low voice. He gesticulated so much that he nearly fell off the ladder. 'We must warn the council! But the council is already meeting for the royal ceremony! I will be hanged if I disturb the royal ceremony!'

'Hurry up, Beta. Time is of the essence,' Arthur reminded him.

'Yes. Of course. Time is of the essence,' the Minimoy repeated, sounding increasingly panicked.

Betameche had made himself dizzy from spinning around so much. He stopped for a second, then jumped down from the ladder and ran to a narrow passageway which resembled a mole's tunnel and was barely higher than he was.

'The king will be so proud of me! But I am going to ruin the ceremony!' Betameche kept repeating as he ran as fast as he could down the tunnel.

The chief of the Bogo-Matassalai approached Arthur and smiled at him.

'You did well.'

'I hope it was enough to convince them!' Arthur replied in a worried voice.

Betameche was still running towards the end of his tunnel. Soon he came into a large hall built into a cave in the ground.

This was the Minimoy village: more than a hundred houses, made of wood and leaves, tangled roots, hollowed-out mushrooms, and dried flowers. Here and there, braided roots served as small bridges connecting the houses to each other. Betameche headed down a large avenue that, at this particular moment, was completely deserted.

Here the architecture was an incredible blanket of vegetation, a patchwork woven by beings who use what exists in nature. Some walls were made of dried earth, others of dandelion stems tied closely to each other, like fences. Dried leaves were generally used as roofing, but some Minimoys preferred wood shavings, arranged like tiles. Low walls, made from pine cone scales, separated some of the houses.

Betameche ran as fast as he could up the lovely avenue, which was lit by streetlamps made of flowers with luminous balls planted at regular intervals. The avenue ended at the council building, an enormous Roman-style amphitheatre dug into the earth, forming a semicircular arena opposite the royal palace.

The entire population of the Minimoys was out in force, and Betameche now had to fight his way through them to reach the council. Using his elbows he pushed people aside, excusing himself as he went, until he finally reached the edge of the arena.

'Oh, no! Right in the middle of the ceremony! They are going to kill me!' he moaned, in a low voice.

In the middle of the empty square stood the stone of the sages, in the centre of which was planted a magic sword.

The weapon was magnificent. It was made of finely chiselled steel engraved with a thousand emblems.

Only half of it was visible. The rest was buried deep in the stone, as if it had been welded there.

In front of the stone, a Minimoy was on one knee, head humbly bowed towards the sacred stone. The Minimoy's face could not be seen, but a few details of clothing indicated to Betameche that it was a warrior. The legs were tied with laces from the feet up to the calves. On the belt were several cutlasses made from mouse teeth and small bags made from the skin of corn kernels.

'Oh, no. They are right at the important part!' Betameche fretted.

The door to the palace opened solemnly. It was a huge door that took up a good portion of the front of the palace. It took four Minimoys to open it completely because it was so heavy and massive.

Two light bearers led the procession out of the palace. These were Minimoys in official dress – all brightly coloured and woven with golden threads. On their heads were hats resembling large transparent balls, each containing a glow-worm. When they advanced, they lit up the way, like torchbearers.

They placed themselves on either side of the platform leading to the square, clearing a passage for the king.

His majesty arrived with a slow and heavy tread. The king was rather large compared to the other

Minimoys, like an adult looming over a child.

His arms were enormous and they reached down as far as his calves. He wore a thick white fur reminiscent of a polar bear and a large beard whose colour blended in with that of the fur.

His face looked ageless, but he was at least two thousand years old. His head seemed surprisingly small in comparison with his body. And funnier, too, buried in his enormous hat covered in bells.

The king advanced to the end of the platform. He was followed by several dignitaries, comprising the rest of the council, who carefully positioned themselves along the sides.

Only one of them stayed close to the king. This was Miro, the mole. His costume would not have been out of place in Shakespeare's *Romeo and Juliet*. He wore small eyeglasses on the end of his nose and had a definitely worried air about him all the time.

The king raised his enormous arms and the crowd cheered him. 'Dear citizens, notables, and dignitaries!' he began in a voice that was old but still strong. 'The wars that our ancestors were forced to wage brought much unhappiness and destruction.' He paused for a moment as if to honour the memory of all those who had perished during that terrible time.

'Thus it was with great wisdom that the sages decided they would no longer wage war, and they buried the sword of power in the stone.' He pointed, with a broad sweep of his arm, to the sword in the stone and the warrior, still on one knee.

'The sword was never to be used again, and we were left to resolve our problems . . . with peaceful methods.'

The crowd seemed to share the king's sentiments. Except, perhaps, for Betameche, who was too anxious about his mission.

The king continued his speech.

'The ancients wrote, on the bottom of the stone, the law that was to govern us: if one day our lands are threatened by an invader, then and only then, a pure heart, motivated by the spirit of justice, knowing neither hatred nor vengeance, may remove the sword of a thousand powers and lead a just battle.'

The king let out a long sigh, full of sadness, before adding, 'Unfortunately, that day has arrived.'

The crowd began to stir as each murmured to his neighbour.

'Our spies have reported that M. the cursed is on the brink of sending a giant army to invade our lands.' A wave of terror flew through the crowd. The first letter of his name was enough to frighten everyone.

'Let us debate!' cried the king, signalling the start of a joyful chaos in which everyone could express themselves without really discussing anything.

'Will this take much longer?' Betameche asked the nearest Minimoy.

The royal guard leaned towards him. 'Oh, yes. Things have only just started!' said the officer. 'We still have the royal summary, the speech of the sages, the warrior's promise, the ratification by the king, and then . . . the opening of the buffet!' he concluded, gleefully.

Betameche began to feel that all was lost. His hands were twisting in all directions, searching for courage.

'People! There is not a moment to spare!' shouted the king, restoring silence.

He is right, thought Betameche. *There is not a moment to spare!*

The king took a few steps towards the warrior, still solemnly bowed before the sword.

'The hour is grave. I suggest that we cut protocol short and immediately call upon the person who seems to me to have all of the qualities needed for this dangerous mission.'

The king took a few steps more. An unexpected benevolence entered his voice.

'This person who, in a few short days, will officially replace me at the head of this kingdom . . .' A childlike smile suddenly made his face seem young. 'I am of course speaking of the Princess Selenia, my daughter.'

He tenderly reached out his arms in the direction of the kneeling warrior. The young girl stood up, revealing her angelic features. Her wild hair, with glints of mauve reflected in the light, was beautifully matched by the turquoise of her almond-shaped eyes.

She was proud and played at being a rebel and a warrior, but her grace betrayed her. She was a real princess, as pale as Snow White, as beautiful as Cinderella, as gracious as Sleeping Beauty, but as crafty as Robin Hood.

It was difficult for the king to hide his pride. The thought that this being was his daughter made him beam.

The crowd applauded wildly. There were few who did so out of broad or deep reflection. They were responding to Selenia's charm, which spread like a breath of air.

The king took one last step towards his daughter.

'Princess Selenia, may the spirit of the ancients guide you,' her father said solemnly.

Selenia came forward, calmly reached for the sword, and was about to place her hand on the hilt when Betameche interrupted.

'Papa!' he cried, elbowing his way through the crowd. Selenia stopped dead in her tracks.

'Beta!' she growled impatiently. Only her little brother was capable of such silly antics at a time like this.

The king searched the crowd for his son.

'Here I am, Papa!' Betameche said, joining a furious Selenia.

'You did this on purpose, didn't you? Couldn't you wait ten seconds before starting your antics?' she snapped.

'I am on a very important mission,' Betameche answered her, as serious as the pope.

'Really? Because my mission *isn't* important? I was about to draw the magic sword to battle against M. the cursed!'

Betameche shrugged. 'You are much too proud and angry to be able to draw that sword, you know.'

'Do tell, Mr Know-It-All!' she replied. 'Do I detect just a bit of jealousy in your words?'

'Not at all!' answered Betameche, lifting his nose skyward.

'All right! Stop squabbling, you two!' said the king, striding up between them. 'Betameche! This is a very important ceremony. I hope that you have a really good reason for interrupting!'

'Yes, Father. The path from the lands above has opened,' Betameche announced.

His words passed quickly through the crowd. An agitated murmur began building.

'Who dared?' cried the king in a terrible voice.

Betameche approached his enormous father.

'His name is Arthur,' he explained timidly. 'He is Archibald's grandson.'

The crowd immediately was in an uproar. The name of Archibald resonated with everyone. The king was rattled.

'And what does this . . . Arthur want?' he asked.

'He wants to speak to the council. He says that a great misfortune is about to befall us and that only he can save us.'

The audience rose up in arms. It was on the verge of panic and rioting. Selenia pushed her brother aside and took his place in front of the king.

'It's true, a great misfortune is coming – it is called M. the cursed and this Arthur has nothing to do with it! It is I, Princess Selenia of the royal family, who will take on the burden of protecting our people.' Without hesitation, she turned and strode over to the sword. She placed her hand on the hilt and tried to pull it out with a graceful gesture.

But grace was apparently of no use, because the sword did not budge. So she tried force, using both her hands.

Nothing happened. The weapon remained one with the stone.

She then used her two hands, her two feet; she contorted herself, grimaced, pulled . . .

Nothing happened. There was confusion in the

crowd and also in the expression of the king, who seemed deeply disappointed and more than a little worried.

Selenia, exhausted, stopped for a second to catch her breath.

'You see: much too proud. I told you so!' Betameche said smugly.

'I'll show you proud!' replied Selenia, leaping down and advancing towards her brother, hands outstretched to strangle him.

'Selenia!' cried her father.

'My dear daughter, I am so sorry,' he said with affection. 'We know how much you love your people but . . . your heart is clearly too full of vengeance for you to draw the sword.'

'That's not true, Father!' she said passionately. 'It's just – Betameche upset me! I am sure that if I calm myself down, in a minute I will be able to pull out the sword and everything will be back in order!'

The king studied her sceptically for a moment. How could he explain to her that her fury was blinding her without breaking her spirit?

'Selenia, answer me this. What would you do if you had M. the cursed right here in front of you?' the king asked her.

Selenia tried to contain her anger, which was demanding to be heard.

'I – I would treat him the way he deserves to be treated,' she asserted.

'And that means?' pressed the king, knowing he was playing on her nerves.

'I . . . I – I would strangle that piece of vermin! For all of the crimes that he has committed and the misfortune he has brought upon us and also for –'

Selenia realized that she had fallen into his trap.

'I am sorry, my daughter, but you are not ready. The powers of the sword act only in hands motivated by justice, not by vengeance,' her father explained to her.

'So what are we going to do? Are we going to allow that creep to invade us, to rob us, to strangle us and our children, too? Without saying a word? Without doing anything? Without trying anything?' she said, addressing the whole crowd.

The assembly was stirred. There was obviously some truth in what the young princess was saying.

'Who is going to save us?' she cried, in conclusion.

'Arthur!' Betameche answered with fervour. 'He is our only hope.'

Selenia rolled her eyes. The king reflected. The crowd wondered.

The council conferred among themselves, and then gave their sovereign a favourable sign. He nodded solemnly.

'Given the circumstances . . . and in memory of

Archibald, the council agrees to hear what this young man has to say.'

Betameche let out a yelp of joy. His sister scowled.

'Miro! Prepare the link!' said the king.

The little mole immediately launched into action. He jumped into his control centre, which was a kind of circular counter filled with protruding handles and knobs of every shape and size.

Miro first did some rapid calculations on his abacus, then pulled handle number 21. An enormous mirror, mounted on roots that served as its frame, emerged from the wall, like a rear-view mirror on a car. A second mirror appeared shortly thereafter, catching the reflection from the first mirror. A third mirror descended from the ceiling and captured its reflection in turn.

Miro engaged the handles one by one and mirrors appeared from everywhere, transporting the same image throughout the town and through the long tunnel leading to where the enormous telescope lens was still planted in the ground.

When it was done, a total of fifty mirrors were lined up to capture the image from the lens.

Miro used two hands to activate a new handle. A plant-like device descended from the ceiling of the cave, opened like a flower, and released four luminous balls: one yellow, one red, one blue, and one green.

These four colours lined themselves up to form a perfect white light, like a large projector ready to faithfully reproduce the image transported by the mirrors.

All that was missing was a screen. Miro pushed on a tab, the only one with a velvet top, and an enormous screen unrolled from the ceiling, filling the sky of the city.

Up close, you could see that it consisted of maple leaves that had been dried and then sewn to each other in a kind of magnificent patchwork. Miro pressed another button. One last mirror made it possible for the reflection to reach the projector, which would then send the image to the enormous screen.

A giant eye filled the screen – Arthur's.

The boy, still on his knees in his garden, couldn't believe it. He was in the middle of the Minimoys' council, face-to-face with the king. The latter was rather impressed by the size of Arthur's eye, which made it possible to imagine the size of the human being behind it.

Selenia turned her back to the screen and folded her arms as a sign of protest.

The king had regained some of his dignity and cleared his throat momentously.

'Hmm! Well, young Arthur, the council will hear you. Please be brief.'

Arthur took a deep breath and announced, 'A bad

man is planning to destroy the garden that shelters you. I have only four more minutes left to pass into your world so I can help you. After that, there is nothing I can do and I'm afraid you will be totally annihilated.'

The news ran through the crowd like a current of air.

The king seemed paralysed.

'That – that *was* brief . . . and precise.'

He turned to the council, who looked as lost as he felt. The king knew he was alone in making this decision.

'Your grandfather was a great and wise man. In his memory, we are going to trust you. Activate the transporter!' he thundered, raising his imposing arms.

Betameche whooped and ran off, bumping into his still-sulking sister as he passed.

Miro pulled a golden handle and an enormous red velvet curtain descended to cover the giant screen.

Chapter 9

Arthur turned towards the chief of the Bogo-Matassalai tribe. 'I think it worked,' he announced timidly.

The warriors did not look surprised.

Betameche bolted down the hall. He rushed up to a silk cocoon hanging from the ceiling.

'Gatekeeper! Gatekeeper! Wake up, it's urgent!' he cried, hammering on the cocoon. There was no reply. Betameche pulled out his multifunction knife and released a bizarre blade – obviously a cocoon cutter. He slit open the silk from one side to the other.

The gatekeeper, who had been sleeping peacefully with his head upside down, slipped through the silky walls and crashed to the ground.

'What in the name of a marshmallow!' the old Minimoy mumbled, rubbing his head. He untangled his long white beard from his legs and smoothed the hair on his ears. 'Who dared to disturb me?'

The old imp recognized the young prince and his face lit up.

'Beta! You good-for-nothing! Can't you find any better way to amuse yourself?'

'My father sent me. We need a passage,' explained the boy, stamping his feet with impatience.

'Again?' complained the gatekeeper. 'Why does everyone want to pass at this very moment?'

'The last passage was four years ago!' Betameche pointed out.

'That's what I was saying! I was just about to fall asleep!' replied the gatekeeper, stretching out.

'Hurry up! The king is impatient!' insisted the prince.

'The king, the king! All right, where is the royal seal?'

Betameche took it out of his pocket and handed it to the gatekeeper.

The gatekeeper took the royal object and inserted it into a box in the wall. 'What about the moon? Is it full tonight? Let's see.'

Muttering to himself, the gatekeeper opened a small trapdoor in the wall, resembling the door to a garbage chute. A mirror was attached to it, reflecting the image of the moon above –imposing, shining, and, above all, full.

'It's beautiful,' murmured the gatekeeper.

'Hurry up!' Betameche cried. 'The beam is getting weaker.'

'Yes, okay! It's okay!' he responded, grumbling.

The gatekeeper moved towards the three rings – the same ones that Arthur had carefully lined up on the other end of the telescope. Except that on this side, for the Minimoys, they seemed enormous.

The gatekeeper seized the first ring.

'Three notches towards the right, for the body,' said the old man, turning it carefully.

He moved to the second ring.

'Three notches to the left, for the mind.'

The second ring turned slowly to the third notch.

The gatekeeper grabbed the third ring.

'And now, one complete turn . . . for the spirit.'

The gatekeeper held the third ring tightly, like a child on a carousel, and turned it.

All at once, the beam that came from the moon changed and began to waver like the horizon line when it is very hot.

'Hold on,' the Bogo-Matassalai chief said to Arthur.

'Hold on? To what?' replied the boy with astonishment.

He had barely asked the question when he began to shrink rapidly, faster than he could even speak.

By instinct, Arthur held on to the lens as he

changed. He put his back up against the glass, all the while continuing to shrink.

'What is happening to me?' he asked, amazed.

'You are going to join our brothers, the Minimoys,' the chief calmly replied. 'But do not forget that you have only sixty hours to fulfil your mission. If you are not back by noon two days from tomorrow, the door will close . . . for a thousand days!' the chief declared firmly.

Arthur nodded his head, which was still shrinking. Behind him, the glass was now as big as the huge oak tree. Suddenly, the lens he was leaning against seemed to become soft, and Arthur sank into it. Then, quite suddenly, he passed right through the glass and fell into the telescope. There he rolled, bouncing like a puppet falling down a flight of stairs.

His fall came to a noisy end as he crashed against the last wall of glass at the end of the telescope, where it stuck into the hall. He rubbed his head as Betameche appeared on his ladder on the other side of the glass.

The two boys seemed equally surprised to see each other. Betameche smiled and made a 'welcome' sign with his hand. Arthur, somewhat stupefied, did the same.

The Minimoy spoke to him and made broad gestures, but the thick glass muffled all conversation. Betameche exaggerated his gestures. He was obviously trying to make Arthur understand something.

'I can't hear you,' Arthur cried, using his hands as a megaphone.

Betameche stood close to the glass and breathed on it to cover it with moisture. On it he drew the picture of a key.

'A key?' said Arthur, making the gesture of turning a key in a lock.

The Minimoy nodded his head. Suddenly Arthur remembered.

'Oh! The key! The one I am always supposed to keep with me!' He dug in his pockets and pulled out the old key, with its tag still attached.

Betameche congratulated him and pointed to a lock on the left wall.

Arthur hesitated, but Betameche gestured his encouragement. So Arthur put in the key and turned.

Immediately, an invisible mechanism was engaged and the ceiling began to descend at an impressive speed. Arthur looked up and saw the glass lens descending towards him.

He was caught in a trap. The ceiling was going to crush him. Arthur was overcome with panic. He banged against the glass and yelled for Beta to help him.

The Minimoy, all smiles, gave him two thumbs up.

Arthur was dumbfounded. He was sure the final seconds of his life were passing. He banged on the glass with all his strength, which did absolutely no good. 'I don't want to die, Beta! Not now! Not like this!' the poor boy hollered helplessly. The ceiling was coming closer and would crush him in a few seconds. Arthur looked Betameche in the eyes, thinking that the last image he would see would be the joyful face of this evil elf.

The glass ceiling reached Arthur's head. He quickly flattened himself against the lens lengthwise.

But the pressure from the glass didn't crush him. Instead it pushed him into the softening glass, so he was suspended like a spoon in a jar of honey. It was impossible to move in this dense and gelatinous substance. All he could do was wait until it spat him out on the other side.

Arthur fell from the lens and crashed to the ground at Betameche's feet, tangled up in hundreds of gelatinous threads, as if he had fallen through a vat of chewing gum.

'Welcome to the land of the Minimoys,' announced the little prince with great joy, his arms wide open.

Arthur got up as best he could, trying to get rid of the threads that were clinging to him. He had not yet realized that he no longer looked like a regular human boy. He had become an authentic Minimoy.

'You frightened me, Beta! I couldn't hear anything, so I thought I was going to die and –' Arthur stopped in mid-sentence.

He had suddenly realized that his arm no longer resembled the one he was accustomed to. Was it possible . . . ?

He got rid of the sticky threads, little by little discovering his Minimoy body. Betameche took him by the shoulders and turned him around so that he could see his reflection in the lens.

Arthur was stunned. He touched his body, then his face, as if to verify that this was not a dream. 'It's incredible,' he finally said.

The gatekeeper looked up from mending his cocoon and smiled. 'Good. You don't need me any more. I am going back to bed.' He climbed back into his cocoon, which he continued to mend from the inside.

Arthur was still hypnotized by his own reflection. 'It's really incredible!'

'You can admire yourself later!' Betameche said, pulling him by the arm. 'The council is waiting for you.'

The chief of the Bogo-Matassalai tribe gently withdrew the telescope from its hole, while his brothers carefully folded the rug with the five points.

The chief looked down the hole one last time.

'Good luck, Arthur,' he said with emotion.

He put the garden gnome back in its place and the little tribe disappeared into the night, as mysteriously as they had come.

The old Chevrolet's motor wheezed to a stop. The light from the headlights faded rapidly and finally went out.

The night once again took over and now the silence was complete . . .

Except for a slight, barely audible humming that came from one of the upstairs bedrooms.

This was most likely Grandma, snoring like a carefree locomotive.

Chapter 10

The king was on his throne, pounding the ground with his sceptre.

'Enter, Arthur!' he boomed in his powerful voice.

The two guards lifted up their swords and opened a way for Arthur, who now had to cross the square under everyone's watchful eyes.

The crowd welcomed him with cries of 'ooh!' and 'ah!' Arthur did his best to hide his embarrassment.

Selenia, her arms still crossed, studied this saviour who had fallen from the sky. He looked more like a chick that had fallen from its nest, she thought. Betameche shot her a sideways glance and nudged her with his elbow.

'Cute, isn't he?' he asked the princess, who shrugged her shoulders.

'Common!' she replied, turning her back on him as

Arthur passed right by her.

'Princess Selenia, my respects,' Arthur managed to say, despite his shyness. He was so afraid that his heart would explode that he could barely look at her. He found her even more beautiful in person. He bowed slightly and continued on his path to the king.

Selenia would never admit it, but his politeness had just earned him several points.

The king was also charmed, but he did not wish to jump to conclusions too quickly. Only Miro the mole was not restrained by protocol. He approached Arthur and vigorously shook his hand.

'I was good friends with Archibald. I am very happy to meet his grandson!' he said, his voice filled with emotion.

Arthur was somewhat embarrassed to find his hand squeezed like a loaf of bread by a mole that he barely knew, but he smiled and nodded as courteously as he could.

'Miro! Leave him be!' said the king, always mindful of good manners.

The little mole pulled himself together and returned to his place. Arthur found himself standing in front of the king, and he bowed to him respectfully.

'Well, my boy, we are listening!' said the king, who was dying of curiosity.

Arthur gathered his courage and began. 'In less than

three days, men will come to tear down the house and the garden. This means that my world, and yours, will be destroyed and covered over with concrete.'

A deathly silence ran through the crowd, like a disagreeable shiver.

'This is a misfortune even greater than that which we feared,' murmured the king.

Selenia could stand it no longer. She turned around and poked Arthur with her finger. 'And you, from your new height of half an inch, you came to save us – is that right?' she tossed out disdainfully.

'The only way to stop these men is to pay them. I think that is why my grandfather came to you four years ago. He was looking for a treasure he'd hidden in the garden that would enable us to pay our debts. I came to complete his mission and to find this treasure,' he explained. It must be said that the mission now seemed much more difficult than it had when he was dreaming in front of drawings, propped up with pillows on his bed.

'Your grandfather was a remarkable man,' conceded the king, lost in his memories. 'He taught us so many things! He was the one who taught Miro how to tame images and light.'

Miro acknowledged this with a sigh full of nostalgia.

The king continued. 'It is true, he came to us looking for his treasure, which was entrusted to us for safekeeping. Sadly, we failed him – the treasure was stolen from us some time ago, and we did not know where it was. And so your grandfather went in search of this famous treasure, and after traversing the seven lands that make up our world, he finally found where it was . . . in the midst of the forbidden lands, at the centre of the kingdom of shadows – in the heart of the city of Necropolis.'

The room shivered as everyone imagined this descent into darkness.

'Necropolis is controlled by a powerful army of fanatically devoted henchmen, all in the grip of their king, who rules as absolute master: the celebrated M. the cursed.'

A few spectators fainted.

'No one has ever returned from the kingdom of shadows,' concluded the king.

'Still ready for this great adventure?' asked Selenia provokingly.

Betameche had had enough, and he stepped in between Arthur and Selenia.

'Leave him alone! He's just learned that he has lost his grandfather. That's hard enough, isn't it?'

The phrase echoed inside of Arthur's head. He hadn't yet clearly understood what the king was saying. His eyes filled with tears. Betameche realized that he had made a mistake.

'Well – I meant to say – we haven't had any news and – no one has ever come back . . . so . . .'

Arthur held back his tears and filled his lungs with courage.

'My grandfather is not dead! I am sure of it!' he said.

The king approached him, uncertain how to deal with the boy's distress. 'My dear Arthur, I am afraid that my son is right. If your grandfather fell into the hands of M. the cursed, or one of the awful henchmen that make up his army, there is little chance that we will ever see him again!'

'Exactly!' Arthur cried. 'M. may be cursed but he is no idiot! What good would it do him to get rid of an old man? None. On the other hand, why not keep a man with such infinite knowledge, a genius capable of solving all kinds of problems?'

The king was obviously intrigued by this hypothesis.

Arthur continued, fired up with excitement. 'I will go to the kingdom of shadows and I will find my grandfather along with the treasure! Even if I have to rescue him from the claws of this evil Maltazard!' he declared in a passion.

The crowd gasped with horror. Arthur had just said the name that was never supposed to be spoken – the name that brings misfortune. And, as everyone knows, misfortune usually comes quickly.

An alarm resounded throughout the city at that exact moment. A guard appeared at the palace door shouting, 'Alert at the main gate!'

There was total panic among the Minimoys. They ran in all directions, they jostled each other, they lost their heads. The king left his throne and quickly headed for the central gate, the main entrance to the town.

Selenia pushed Arthur's shoulder. He was confused at having set off such an uproar.

'You really made an entrance!' the princess said to him angrily. 'Didn't anyone tell you that you must never pronounce that name?'

Poor Arthur was wringing his hands. 'Yes, but –'

'But the fine gentleman still does whatever he feels like doing – is that it?' She stormed off without giving him time to explain or even to apologize.

The entire Minimoy populace clustered around the central gate, and the guards had to use their nightsticks to clear a passage for the king and his two children. Miro pulled a handle and a little mirror appeared above them, a bit like a periscope. The mole looked up and observed what was happening on the other side of the gate.

A long pipe, like a giant avenue leading to the entrance, stretched before him, out to infinity. Everything seemed calm.

Miro turned the mirror slightly to check the sides of the pipe.

All at once, a hand appeared on the mirror. A cry of astonishment resounded through the crowd. Miro turned the wheel of the mirror to lower the image. Then they all saw a Minimoy, lying on the ground outside in very bad shape.

'It's Gandolo! The ferryman from the great river!' cried a guard in recognition. The king leaned towards the mirror to have a better view. 'Incredible! We thought he was lost for ever in the forbidden lands!' he said, amazed.

'I guess that proves that you *can* come back!' Selenia responded.

'Yes, but in what condition! Open the doors quickly!' the king ordered.

Arthur cast a worried glance towards the mirror as the guards slid back the large beams that blocked the door. Something had caught his eye – on the bottom, on the right side of the image. Something strange, like a corner becoming detached.

'Stop!' he cried.

Everyone froze in place.

The king turned towards the boy and gave him a questioning look.

'Sire, look! It looks like something out there is coming unglued.'

The king looked for himself. 'Why . . . yes, it does. But I'm sure it's nothing serious. We can glue it back later,' he said, without understanding.

'Sir, you don't understand! That's a painted canvas! It's a trap! My grandfather used this method in Africa to protect himself from ferocious beasts!' Arthur explained.

'But we are not ferocious beasts!' Selenia remarked. 'And we are certainly not going to let this poor unfortunate soldier die! Besides, if he has returned from the forbidden lands, he must have many things to tell us! Open the gates!' she ordered.

Outside, Gandolo was crawling along the ground, his hand outstretched in front of him. 'Don't open the gate! It's a trap!' he rasped under his breath.

Of course, no one heard Gandolo's plea, and the guards began to open the heavy gate. However, they still hesitated to run to the rescue of the poor ferryman, out in the open, exposed pipe.

Only Selenia stepped forward, ready to brave the unknown danger.

'Be careful, my child,' insisted her father, whose size was much larger than his courage.

'If any henchmen were waiting to attack, we would see them coming for miles!' replied the Princess with great courage.

At first glance, the enormous empty pipe did seem

to extend infinitely into the clear distance. But only at first glance. Arthur was convinced that this was really a trap, into which his favourite princess was about to fall.

'Don't do it, Princess Selenia,' Gandolo murmured, but nobody heard him.

Arthur couldn't stand it any more. He grabbed a torch from one of the guards and threw it with all his might. The flaming torch flew over Selenia's head and crashed headlong into a painted canvas stretched across the pipe that, up to then, had been invisible.

The crowd was dumbfounded. Arthur was right! Selenia couldn't believe her eyes. The torch fell to the ground and immediately set fire to the gigantic canvas, which flared up like a piece of straw.

'Oh, no!' Selenia cried, watching the wall of flames consume the canvas. Arthur shot past at full speed and grabbed Gandolo by the legs.

'Selenia, come on! We have to get him out of here!' Arthur yelled over the noise of the flames. The princess woke from her state of shock and grabbed the injured man under the arms.

'Close the gates!' ordered the king in a frightened voice.

Arthur and Selenia ran as best they could, weighed down by poor Gandolo's body. The canvas was almost entirely consumed when the last large piece fell to the ground, revealing an army of M.'s horrible henchmen.

The fire was still too intense to cross, and the henchmen were impatiently lunging forward on the other side of the frame. There were about one hundred of these evil insects, each one uglier than the next. Each wore armour made from the shells of rotten walnuts.

M.'s henchmen carried all kinds of weapons, mainly swords. For battle, they had brought with them the famous 'tears of death', drops of oil held together by braided cords and attached to the end of a sling. The cord was lit, the drop was tossed, and a tongue of fire would spread over everything in sight.

Each henchman had his own mount – mosquitoes, trained and harnessed for war.

The chief henchman saw the gates closing and decided to begin the assault despite the intensity of the fire. He lifted his sword in the air and let out an unearthly cry.

In chorus, one hundred henchmen joyously echoed him.

'Hurry up, Selenia,' yelled Arthur, as the gates were fast closing and the first mosquitoes passed over his head. Selenia called on all her strength, and together the three of them tumbled inside.

The king threw himself against the door and, with powerful arms, finished the work of the guards.

Several mosquitoes crashed into the gate as the guards were bolting the safety bars. Unfortunately, a dozen henchmen on mosquitoes had managed to enter the city and were already circling in the air.

There was panic everywhere, as each Minimoy tried to reach his battle station.

The henchmen had raised their tears of death and were whirling them around over their heads. The mosquitoes swooped down like bombs and the balls of fire exploded on the ground, leaving an immense trail that consumed everything in its way.

'We have to fight, Arthur! Until the end!' Betameche proudly cried.

'I would like to, but with what?' Arthur called back.

'Here!' said Betameche, giving him his stick. 'I'm going to look for another weapon!'

Betameche took off, leaving Arthur with his stick.

The henchmen did a dance of triumph in the air above, punctuating each step with a falling bomb.

Out of nowhere, a fierce ball of fire swooped down and hit the king from behind. The Minimoy stumbled and fell to the ground – in two pieces!

Arthur let out a cry of horror before he realized the sovereign was unhurt. Selenia rolled her eyes and went to help her father up as Palmito, his faithful malbak, got up on his own.

Palmito was a large furry animal with a flat head,

which was practical for attaching him to the king's throne. It was this creature who served as the body of the king in order to provide him with the strength and assurance required of royalty – because, in reality, the king was nothing but a little old man, even smaller than his daughter, who gently dusted him off.

'Are you okay?' the king asked his faithful companion.

Palmito nodded and smiled sheepishly, as if to apologize for falling over so easily.

'Go hide in the palace!' the king said to him. 'Your big, beautiful fur is too much of a target for the tears of death!'

The malbak seemed hesitant to leave his master.

'Hurry up! Now!' the king ordered him.

Palmito disappeared into the palace.

For a moment, the king watched the disaster that was overtaking the city and the mosquitoes' aerial ballet overhead.

'Organize the counter-attack!' cried the king.

Everyone grabbed what they could to put out the fires that were blazing throughout the city. Mothers collected their children and slid them down safety hatches that were designed for that very purpose.

On the left flank, a dozen Minimoys mounted a kind of home-made catapult.

The chief of the operation put on his helmet and sat down in his shooting seat. He activated the viewfinder in front of him. A cartridge began releasing raisins one by one into a wooden spoon connected to a complex system of springs.

The chief tracked a mosquito in his viewfinder, then released the trigger. A raisin was launched into the air, but it missed its mark. Automatically, the cartridge released another raisin into the spoon.

Miro had returned to his position controlling the mirrors. He checked his system of levers by consulting his abacus.

The head marksman launched another raisin that, unfortunately, missed its target yet again. The henchman, annoyed at having been shot at like a pigeon, dived towards the catapult and fired a tear of death. Luckily he also missed his target, but the explosion sent Arthur flying. He landed heavily on a raisin that had just been released into the catapult.

The chief marksman did not see him, as he was too absorbed with targeting the mosquito in his viewfinder.

'No, wait!' yelled Arthur, suddenly aware of his dangerous position.

The chief activated his valve and the raisin shot into the sky, with Arthur aboard clinging on for dear life. The projectile shot through the air over the city, heading straight for one of the mosquitoes.

'Did you see that? It's Arthur! He's flying!' marvelled the marksman.

'You're the one that shot him into the air, imbecile!' replied his superior.

The henchman saw the raisin hurtling towards him just in time to duck and narrowly avoid it. But then Arthur leaped onto the mosquito's back, throwing the creature off balance for a moment.

The henchman turned to check the damage and spotted Arthur behind him, holding on as best he could. Terrified and trying not to show it, the boy thrust his stick in front of him and assumed a wicked look.

The warrior smiled menacingly and took out a monstrous sword, made of steel. He stood up on his mount and advanced towards Arthur with the clear intention of cutting him in two.

Arthur tried, as best he could, to stand up, too, but it wasn't easy on a mosquito that was zooming through the air like a rocket ship.

The warrior raised his arm and lunged at Arthur with all his might.

The boy ducked at the last minute, and the henchman's arm, pulled by the weight of the sword, twisted around his neck and half suffocated him. He teetered for a moment, then suddenly lost his balance and fell, to Arthur's great surprise.

Now Arthur was left to take command of the creature. He grabbed a rein in each hand and tried not to panic.

'Okay! This can't be any more complicated than Grandma's car!' he said to himself nervously. 'To move to the left – probably all you have to do is pull to the left.'

Arthur lightly pulled the left rein. The mosquito immediately flipped over and began to fly upside down.

Arthur let out a yell and caught hold of the ends of the reins just in time to avoid plummeting to the ground. The creature flew every which way, confused by the mixed signals it was getting. It took off in a mad frenzy, skimming the ground above the city.

'Watch out, Beta,' Arthur screamed, a hair's breadth away from knocking his friend out with his dangling legs. Betameche threw himself down on the ground, but Arthur and his mosquito were already climbing back into the air.

Almost immediately, another henchman began to give chase.

Miro saw it and turned his seat in the direction of the two mosquitoes as they flew into a tunnel. Arthur, still hanging from the ends of the reins, guided the creature as best he could. Behind him, the henchman had unsheathed his sword and was brandishing it over his head.

Miro identified their paths and pressed a button. A mirror sprang out suddenly from the wall of the tunnel, just as Arthur shot past. His pursuer was smacked in the face, and stopped dead in his tracks.

Another henchman, who saw what happened to his colleague, flew up to the ceiling of the tunnel and began skimming along it.

'Pay attention to the walls,' he screamed to his comrades-in-arms. 'There are traps in the walls! Fly closer to the ceiling, it's saf –'

He didn't have time to complete his sentence. Miro released a mirror from the ceiling, the way a fighter releases an uppercut, and the henchman crashed headlong into it. The shock was so violent that he was thrown from his mount, which flew on without him.

Meanwhile, Betameche, completely winded, had crossed the city carrying his little cage. He stopped several yards inside the tunnel that led to the door of light.

He caught his breath for a moment and then let out a beautiful whistle. On the other side of town, the waiting soldier heard the signal and opened the other cage. The mul-mul immediately took off in search of its partner.

The little creature spun wildly through the air for a moment, like a dog that is not sure of its sense of smell. Finally, it found its direction and sped upward, above the city. The white ball zoomed past a mosquito, which immediately changed direction, much to the surprise of its rider.

'What are you doing, you idiot?' the henchman hollered at his mount.

A mul-mul is possibly a mosquito's favourite food in the world. The henchman could pull on the reins all he wanted, but nothing could stop the creature now. An empty stomach has no ears.

'But it's not time to eat, you six-legged cretin!'

The mosquito ignored the insults. All it could see was an appetizing white ball – that was leading it to the mouth of the narrow tunnel.

'No!' cried the henchman, realizing the trap he had fallen into.

The mul-mul was zooming towards the tunnel to rejoin its mate, and the mosquito was prepared to demolish anything in its way in order to follow . . . including itself.

As the warrior and his mount smashed into the tunnel wall, Betameche opened his cage and the mul-mul was reunited with its mate, who lovingly threw herself into his arms. (Of course, this is just an expression, since mul-muls have no arms.)

'Well done, my lovebirds!' said Betameche, as he dashed off to return to his position.

Arthur hung from the ends of the reins, pursued by yet another henchman. The warrior had bared his sword and was preparing to cut our hero into slices like a sausage.

The henchman approached, his sword swinging in the air. Arthur prepared himself for the end. The warrior struck with a mighty blow. Arthur lifted his legs out of the way, and the sword got caught in the reins.

'Sorry,' called Arthur, who was always polite, regardless of the circumstances.

Furious, the henchman tried to untangle his sword by pulling upward. The mosquito interpreted this sudden movement as a change of direction and reared up angrily. The henchman, clinging to his sword, was torn off his mount.

Arthur lost his balance, let go of the reins, fell, and landed on the back of his pursuer's mosquito. Arthur's spirits rose as he grabbed the reins and rolled them around his stick.

'Good work, Arthur!' he reassured himself, plucking up his courage.

This time, he pulled very slowly on the leather strap, and the mosquito executed a magnificent wide turn to the left. The centrifugal force was impressive, but Arthur held on.

'Wow! That's it, I've got it! The battle is mine!' he cried fervently. Just then a raisin hit him right in the face. He lost control of his mosquito, momentarily stunned by the shot.

'I got him!' the marksman shouted triumphantly, leaning over the side of the catapult.

'That's Arthur you've unseated, idiot!' the chief retorted furiously.

Arthur and his uncontrollable monster were nose-diving into another henchman, who was brandishing a tear of death.

'Watch out!' Arthur cried to the henchman, who could not see the catastrophe that was about to befall him from above.

The two mounts smashed into each other, and the tear of death exploded on Arthur's mosquito.

Fortunately, Arthur had had the clever idea of jumping into the void before the collision. Given his new size, he felt like he was falling from a height of about a hundred feet.

Luckily, he once again landed on a mosquito without a rider.

He was saved, with only one small problem: he had landed sitting backward, so it was impossible to see where his new mount was taking him.

Meanwhile, his former mount had caught fire and was in a nose-dive, headed directly towards the king. Selenia saw it coming.

'Watch out!' she cried, throwing herself at her father. The old man tripped under the weight of his daughter, who threw herself over him like a blanket.

The mosquito hit the ground and exploded in a long trail of fire.

'Are you all right, Father?' a worried Selenia immediately asked.

'I will be all right,' replied the king, visibly weakened. 'But for the moment I think I would prefer to remain here on the ground. There's a better view of the show from here,' he joked, feeling himself incapable of getting up for the moment. Selenia smiled at him and remained at his side, prepared to defend him with her life.

After a series of complex acrobatics, Arthur managed to turn himself around so he was now facing forward. He grabbed the reins one more time and gave a couple of small tugs. The mosquito reacted better than a Ferrari and began to chase after a henchman.

The king spotted him flying overhead.

'Selenia! Look!' he said to his daughter.

The young princess searched the skies for a moment and noticed Arthur's pursuit. She was struck speechless, torn between jealousy and amazement.

Arthur managed to guide his mount directly above the henchman's. He cleared his throat to attract the warrior's attention. The latter looked up and saw Arthur. He was also struck speechless.

'Need some ammunition?' the boy asked. Then he pulled on the cord that was holding back all of his mount's tears of death. The henchman tried as best he could to catch the first ones, but he was like a skier confronted by an avalanche. He quickly lost control of his mosquito, and together they smashed against the wall.

'Arthur!' cried Selenia, her hands over her face.

Arthur made a very tight turn in order to avoid the collision, just like a real fighter pilot, then triumphantly flew to safety.

'What bravura! What audacity!' commented the king. 'It's amazing how much he resembles me!' He realized he'd spoken aloud. 'Er, what I meant to say is, I was very like that at his age – valiant, vigorous, valorous –'

'And virtuous?' his daughter shot back.

Arthur was proud as a peacock as he controlled his mosquito. 'Who should we tackle next?' he asked, just as a mul-mul whizzed by.

His mosquito was immediately hypnotized and spun around to pursue its favourite dish. Arthur was almost thrown from his mount by the violence and suddenness of the turn.

'What's gotten into you?' Arthur wondered, realizing that he had not yet learned all the secrets of a mosquito. Even though he pulled the reins in all directions, nothing happened. His mosquito was determined not to stop until it had taken a nice bite out of the mul-mul.

Betameche was awaiting his prey at the end of the narrow passage, when he spotted poor Arthur, trapped on the mosquito and heading straight for the tunnel.

'Oh, no! Not him!' cried Betameche, paralysed with fear.

Miro saw the scene from afar. He pivoted his seat and prepared to attempt a rescue.

'The poor thing! He is going to crash!' cried the terrified king.

Even Selenia seemed to be worrying about Arthur, for once.

'Arthur! *Jump!*' Betameche shouted to him.

The boy didn't hear. He pulled so hard on the reins that they came loose. He slid back and, despite all his scrambling, fell off the creature into thin air.

'Arthur!' cried Selenia, her hands over her face.

It was a miracle. Arthur was hanging from a bit of root jutting out of the ceiling.

The mul-mul shot into the little tunnel and the mosquito, which was still following it, crashed into the walls and ended up flat as a pancake.

Chapter 11

Selenia let out a sigh of relief that betrayed her. She turned towards her father and caught him smiling at her. He had discerned his daughter's true feelings for Arthur. Feeling exposed, she gave her father a very sharp look.

'What?' she snapped, as cold as ice.

'I didn't say anything!' replied the king innocently, lifting his arms above his head as if he had just been arrested.

From his control seat, Miro was also smiling as he watched the small slip of a boy landing safely.

'I really like this boy!' he chortled to himself.

Betameche ran over to stand beneath Arthur.

'Arthur! Are you okay?' he asked.

'Perfect!' the boy replied, utterly exhausted. He had barely finished uttering the word when the root he was clutching stretched to its limit, and then tore.

Arthur let out a cry that seemed unending – like his fall.

But Miro was on the ball. He activated his levers quickly, one after another. A mirror emerged from the wall and caught Arthur, who slid onto a second mirror that appeared just below that. The sliding continued to a third mirror, then a fourth. Miro opened the mirrors one by one and Arthur slid down at full speed, as if he were going downstairs on his behind.

The boy bounced from one mirror to another and ended up in a heap on the dusty ground.

Miro was relieved, as was the king. And so was Selenia, although she would never admit it.

His back aching, Arthur reached for his stick and used it to help himself stand up. From a distance he looked like a little old man leaning on his cane.

'You're right, Dad! It's amazing how he resembles you!' Selenia said jokingly.

Betameche came to the aid of his friend.

'Are you okay? Nothing broken?' the Minimoy asked with concern.

'I don't know. I can't feel my behind any more!'

Betameche giggled.

The sky above the city was now clear; most of the mosquitoes had been downed. But two still remained, and these swooped down to land at the king's feet.

Selenia instinctively placed herself in front of her father. The two henchmen dismounted and unsheathed their swords.

'Don't worry. It's not the king that we want – it's you!' the henchman sneered.

'You won't have either one of us!' the princess bravely replied, reaching for her dagger. The henchmen sneered some more, and then rushed towards her with a yell.

Charging and yelling are probably the only two things that a henchman knows how to do well. The battle was an unequal one. Selenia managed a few passes with her dagger, and was able to beat them back briefly, but a well-aimed blow sent her dagger spiralling through the air.

Then she was on the ground, at the mercy of the two sinister warriors.

'Go ahead, grab her!' said one of them.

'Hey!' yelled a voice from behind them. The two henchmen turned around and discovered Arthur, armed with his trusty stick.

'Pick on somebody your own size!' Arthur said, tightening his hands around his poor stick.

'Do you see someone our size around here?' one of the henchmen said, glancing around.

'No!' his colleague replied, giggling.

Arthur, offended, filled his lungs with air and

charged at the henchmen, his stick leading the way.

The warrior drew his sword with lightning speed and severed Arthur's stick level with Arthur's hand. The boy stopped short.

'You finish him off. I'll take care of the girl,' said the other henchman darkly.

Arthur fell back, avoiding, as best he could, the powerful blows of the sword.

Selenia stuck to her father's side, ready to sacrifice her life for him. But the henchman cared nothing about sacrifices. All he wanted was to capture the princess.

Arthur was furious, frustrated, and overwhelmed by all these injustices. Wasn't there any divine protection from evil? Why didn't adults do anything to help, with all their big talk about justice, good and evil? he wondered.

He tripped on a large stone and his hand landed on the hilt of the magic sword. Was this a sign from above?

Arthur didn't know. The only thing he did know was that a sword would be much more useful in his hand than in the stone. Arthur grasped the sword and pulled it out, as if sliding it out of butter.

The king couldn't believe his eyes. Selenia's jaw dropped.

'A miracle!' cried Miro in awe.

The two henchmen looked at Arthur with suspicion,

wondering how he had managed this magic trick. But, since all thinking, for a henchman, leads back to violence, the two warriors resumed their attack.

Arthur lifted his sword and began to fight. To his great surprise, the sword seemed light to him. He fought with grace and lightness, as if he were in a dream.

Betameche approached Miro.

'Where did he learn to fight like that?' the little prince wondered.

'It is the sword that gives him this power,' Miro replied. 'It multiplies the strength of the just.'

The two henchmen quickly exhausted all of their moves. Arthur pressed harder, and with each new exchange he cut a bit off the henchmen's swords. Very soon, the two warriors were left with nothing but hilts in their hands.

Arthur took advantage of the moment to catch his breath and to smile a victor's smile.

'Now, down on your knees!' he declared, threatening them with the point of his sword.

Selenia advanced slowly and stood in front of the two warriors, who knelt with their heads bowed.

'We're sorry . . .' said the first.

'Princess,' finished the second.

Selenia lifted her chin, as only a princess can.

'Guards! Take the prisoners to the retraining centre!'

ordered the king. A few guards appeared and led off the two henchmen.

'What is a retraining centre?' asked Arthur.

'It is a necessary evil,' the old king answered. 'I don't like to subject anyone to it, but it is for their own good. After the shock treatment they will go back to what they were before they became evil insects: simple, gentle Minimoys.'

Arthur watched the prisoners go, his throat tightening at the thought of the ordeal that awaited them.

Betameche ran up to Arthur, his face alight with amazement.

'You fought like a chief! It was incredible!'

'It's this sword, not me. It's so light, everything seemed easy!' Arthur modestly explained.

'Of course – it's a magic sword! It has been in the stone for years, and you are the only one who was able to draw it!' announced Betameche with great excitement.

'Really?' asked Arthur, examining his sword.

The king approached, a paternal smile on his lips.

'Yes, Arthur! You are a hero now. Arthur the hero!'

Wild with joy, Betameche began to yell. 'Long live Arthur the hero!'

The Minimoys, who were slowly returning to the square, began to cheer as they chanted the name of their hero. Arthur raised his arms in a timid wave, visibly embarrassed by his sudden popularity.

Selenia took advantage of the general euphoria to distract her father. 'Now that the sword has been removed from the stone, there is not a moment to lose! I ask your permission to undertake my quest, Father.'

The king gazed at the jubilant crowd. They were happy and carefree now, but he couldn't help but wonder how long this moment of peace could last. He gave his daughter a look of deep affection.

'Unfortunately, my daughter, I agree with you. This mission must be undertaken and you are the only one among us who will be able to lead it to a successful conclusion. However, I do have one condition,' he added, enjoying the suspenseful moment.

'What is it?' asked the princess.

'Arthur is brave and valorous. His heart is pure and his cause is just. He shall accompany you.'

His tone was unmistakable. Any discussion would be useless and Selenia knew it. She lowered her eyes and accepted her father's decision without argument, which was fairly unusual, for her.

'I am proud of you, my daughter,' her father exclaimed. 'I am sure that you two will make an excellent team!'

Only an hour earlier, the princess would have considered this remark a horrible insult. But Arthur had fought bravely and he had saved her father. There was something else, too, although she would never admit it: a little door had opened inside her heart, and somehow Arthur had slipped through.

Arthur could feel that something had changed, but he would have to live a while longer before he'd be able to define it. He smiled shyly at Selenia, as if to apologize for having been imposed on her.

Selenia's eyes narrowed, like those of a cat when it purrs, and she gave him a radiant smile in return.

The central gate of the city creaked open slowly. A guard stuck his head out and slowly advanced. He shot a flaming arrow. The projectile landed on the ground, some distance away. There was no painted canvas this time.

'The route is clear,' called the guard, turning towards the gate, which was now opened wide. All of the Minimoy people were there to bid one last goodbye to their princess and their new hero.

Arthur slid the sword into a magnificent leather sheath that the Minimoys had given him. Miro laid a gentle hand on his shoulder.

'I know that you are going to look for your grandfather, but –' Miro paused, fidgeted, and then continued hurriedly. 'But if, during your search, you should encounter a little mole wearing glasses who answers to the name Milo . . . that's my son. He has been gone for three months . . . probably the henchmen . . .' Miro broke off and lowered his head, as if sadness had made it too heavy for him to bear.

'We will watch for him. You can count on me,' Arthur said without hesitation.

The old mole smiled, amazed by the young hero's energy and good heart.

'Thank you, Arthur. You're a good boy,' he replied.

A short distance away, Betameche was preparing to put on his backpack. Two guards lifted the enormous bag, while the prince slid his arms through the shoulder straps.

'Are you sure you haven't forgotten anything?' joked one of the guards.

'I'm sure. Okay, let it go!'

The two guards, already panting with exhaustion, let go of the pack. Betameche fell back under its weight, landing on the ground like a turtle on its back.

The two guards doubled over with laughter, as did the king. Selenia sighed heavily.

'Father, does Beta really have to come with us? I'm sure he is going to slow us down, and we have so little time as it is!'

'Even though he is still young, Beta is the prince of this kingdom, and one day it may be his turn to rule!' the king answered. 'He also deserves this chance to prove his bravery and to learn from the experience.'

Selenia scowled, proving that she was still her old self.

'Fine! We'd better get going,' she said, turning on her heels and striding away without kissing her father goodbye. 'Let's go!' she called to Arthur as she marched past him.

Arthur waved goodbye to Miro and caught up with Selenia. Betameche looked up from where he was removing objects from his pack and saw his sister leaving.

'Hey! Wait for me!' he cried, putting his backpack on again without taking the time to close it. He ran to catch up with his comrades, leaving a trail of items clattering to the ground behind him.

Selenia was already in the immense tunnel that led out of the city. Betameche caught up with her, gasping.

'You could have waited for me!' he complained.

'Excuse us – we have a country of people to save!' the princess retorted acidly.

The three continued into the darkness of the tunnel. Only the torch that Arthur was carrying dimly lit the way, forming a small ball of light around the three heroes.

Behind them, the Minimoy people were waving their last goodbyes as the guards closed the heavy gates with a muffled boom.

The king sighed.

'I hope they'll be able to avoid the henchmen!' he said to Miro in a low voice. 'And speaking of henchmen, how are our prisoners?'

'They are stubborn, but we are making progress,' the mole answered.

The two henchmen in question had had their armour removed and were soaking in a large bathtub filled with multicoloured bubbles. Beautiful Minimoys were blowing bubbles in various shapes around the room, while others danced nearby to a rhythmic tune. The ambience was warm, sweet, and intoxicating, enough to soften even the two chunks of granite that were these henchmen's hearts.

Two charming Minimoys approached and offered them drinks.

'No!' they replied in unison.

The painful process of retraining had begun.

Chapter 12

The tunnel in which our three adventurers were walking now seemed colder, darker, and more threatening. Everywhere the walls were oozing, and each drop that fell from the ceiling hit the ground noisily like bombs being dropped from the sky.

'Selenia, I'm a little scared!' said Betameche, sticking close to his sister.

'So stay home! We'll tell you all about it when we return!' she replied with her natural scornfulness. 'Do you want to turn back, too?' she asked Arthur.

'Not for anything in the world!' he replied without hesitation. 'I want to stay with you – I mean . . . to protect you!'

Selenia rolled her eyes, seized the sheath from his hands, and buckled it to her belt. 'Don't worry about me. I can protect myself!' she said, adjusting the magic sword.

'But it's thanks to Arthur that the sword was released from the stone!' cried Betameche.

'So?' the princess replied nonchalantly.

'Well, the least you could do is thank him!'

'Thank you, Arthur, for releasing the *royal* sword which, as its name indicates, can be worn only by the *royal* family. You're not king yet, as far as I know.'

'Um . . . no,' a somewhat confused Arthur replied.

'So then I am the one who should carry it!' she said, speeding up. The two boys exchanged dismayed glances. It wouldn't be easy travelling with her attitude.

'We are going to the surface to take a transporter. It will save time!' the princess added. Selenia climbed onto a joint in the tunnel and pulled herself up through a small hole towards the surface.

The three emerged into a forest of tall grass, thick, immense, and almost impenetrable. Of course, to a human-sized person, it was just a small patch of grass, somewhere in the middle of the garden opposite the house.

The second-floor window was still open. A gentle spring breeze brushed across Grandma's cheek as she struggled to awaken from her deep sleep.

'I slept like a log!' she said in a hoarse voice, rubbing the back of her neck.

She put on her slippers and shuffled to Arthur's

room. She did not remember that she had locked it only hours before as she turned the knob and peered through the doorway.

The shape of Arthur was bundled under the covers, curled up in the middle of the bed, completely hidden from view. She withdrew with a smile and gently closed the door.

Grandma opened the front door and brought in the two bottles of milk left on the steps – proof that Davido had not yet taken control of the dairy, at least.

This good sign encouraged her to look up and appreciate the beautiful day that had just begun. A blue sky paraded over the cheerful garden and the magnificent trees. Magnificent except for one, that is, which appeared to be in a rather sorry state – the one with the front of a Chevrolet wrapped around its trunk like a scarf.

Grandma started with horror. 'What on earth? Did I forget the emergency brake again?' she wondered aloud.

Meanwhile our three heroes were advancing at a healthy pace. They had to be moving at least five hundred inches an hour.

Selenia followed the path as easily as if it were her own garden.

'Selenia? Could you slow down a little, please?' her brother pleaded.

'Absolutely not! It's your own fault – you didn't have to load yourself down like a gamoul!'

'I took a little bit of everything, just in case,' Betameche replied breathlessly.

Arthur looked up and saw that Selenia was heading for a centipede who, given their size, was charging towards them like an enormous truck. The creature looked gigantic, with a thousand legs as big as bulldozers. But Selenia continued her route straight towards the monster as if she hadn't seen it.

'Beta – do you have something "just in case" we come across a thing like that?' asked Arthur, who was pretty close to panicking.

'Don't worry!' Betameche answered, taking something out of his pocket. 'I have my knife. It has three hundred functions! I got it for my birthday.'

The little prince proudly exhibited his treasure, which looked vaguely like a Swiss army knife, and described its functions.

'See here: a rotating saw, double knife, multiheaded pliers. And there: soap bubbler, music box, and waffle iron. On this side: seed opener, eight-perfume injector, surface vanillier, and for when it is too hot – the fan!' Betameche pressed the button and a magnificent Japanese fan appeared. The little prince immediately began to fan himself, as if bothered by the heat.

'That's funny. For my birthday last year, I got the same

thing – well, not exactly!' Arthur answered, keeping an eye on the centipede moving towards them. 'So . . . do you have anything for centipedes?' he added anxiously.

'There are all the classics, too!' continued Betameche without really listening. 'There's the tulipod, machete, fixomats, gulpers and grinders, hole pluggers, a welding nautilus, an acorn-driver –'

Selenia, who had heard just about enough, cut him off. 'Is there *anything* that can make you shut up?' she said, drawing the magic sword. Betameche shrugged as Selenia advanced towards the centipede and began to slice its legs as if she were harvesting wheat.

The creature reared up, almost choking on the grass it was nibbling. Our three heroes strolled underneath the centipede as if they were travelling down a supermarket aisle. The centipede took off in the opposite direction, and with all those feet it raised quite a cloud of dust.

Arthur stood still and watched the gigantic animal pass over his head like an aeroplane taking off. Betameche didn't even look up from his knife.

'Then here, on the last side, there are all the new functions, like the frilled puller, which is very practical for hunting the plumed badarou.'

'What kind of bird is that, a badarou?' asked Arthur, his eyes riveted on the centipede's belly.

'It's a fish,' Betameche replied. 'I also have a white

grape peeler, a raisin humidifier, a toad launcher, a kaflon protector, and a series of fist weapons: the para-abacus, the antigisette, a twelve-shot sifflon, the brand-new double-faced karkanon . . .'

The centipede had disappeared, leaving a cloud of dust and a relieved Arthur behind.

'And, last but not least!' concluded Betameche, 'the final function, my favourite: the comb!' He pressed a button that released a small tortoiseshell comb. The prince combed the three hairs on his head with genuine delight.

'That's one I don't have,' said Arthur with a grin.

The central station, a crossroads for all travellers, was built on ground that was pretty much clear of trees. From a distance, it looked like a flat stone placed on the ground. Closer up, one could see that in fact two stones had been placed one on top of the other.

There was also an enormous counter that could accommodate several dozen passengers at a time. But today, the counter was hopelessly empty.

Selenia approached the large stone on which the following could be read:

EXPRESSO-TRANSPORTATION OF ALL KINDS

'Is anyone here?' Selenia asked no one in particular.

There was no reply. But the gates were open and torches were lit inside the offices.

'So, not too many people travel here, in your country,' Arthur noted as he looked around.

'Once you have taken one voyage, you will understand why!' Betameche answered sarcastically.

Arthur didn't like the sound of that, but his attention was drawn to a half-ball, placed on the counter. It very closely resembled the kind of bell found at hotel front desks, so Arthur decided to try pressing it.

The object turned out to be an animal, which immediately started shrieking. The creature extended its feet, revealing its babies, sleeping under its shell. The mother scolded him in an unknown language, most likely cricket.

'I – I am so sorry! I thought you were a bell!' said an embarrassed Arthur.

The creature looked even more offended and began howling once again.

'No, no, I meant to say: I didn't know that you were alive!' Arthur was in even deeper trouble now. The mother harrumphed several times and moved off along the counter, followed by her brood.

'That won't do, knocking out the clientele like that!' said an old Minimoy who had just appeared behind the counter. His little overalls were made from cornflower petals and his large moustache was as hairy as his ears.

'I am really sorry,' said Arthur.

Selenia came up to the window, cutting the conversation short.

'Excuse me, but we have no time to waste. I am the Princess Selenia!' she proclaimed.

The old employee closed an eye to squint at her.

'Ah! I see! And is that imbecile over there your brother?'

'Exactly!' Selenia replied before Betameche could open his mouth.

'And who is the third joker, the one assaulting my customers?' grumbled the Minimoy, obviously in a bad mood.

'My name is Arthur,' the boy answered politely. 'I am looking for my grandfather.'

The employee seemed intrigued. He began to think.

'You know, I transported a grandfather a few years ago . . . what the devil was his name . . . ?'

'Archibald?' suggested Arthur.

'Archibald! Yes, that's it!'

'Do you know where he went?' asked Arthur, his eyes full of hope.

'Yes, I remember it well. The old eccentric demanded that I send him to Necropolis! Right into the midst of the henchmen! The poor fool!' he commented.

'That's great!' Arthur exclaimed. 'That's exactly where we want to go!'

The agent stood still for a moment, shocked by this response. All at once he slammed his window with a bang, bringing down the gate.

'That's too bad. It's full!' he said.

Selenia didn't have time for this. She took out her sword, thrust it through the counter and cut out a hole. She pushed open the newly sawn-out door, which fell to the ground with a crash.

The employee stood frozen at the back of his office, his moustache vertical with fear.

'What time is the next departure for Necropolis?' demanded the princess.

Betameche had already taken a master schedule out of his pack. It was at least eight hundred pages long.

'The next train leaves in eight minutes!' he said, finding the page. 'And it's an express!'

Selenia took out a little purse full of coins and threw it at the employee's feet.

'Three tickets for Necropolis! First-class, please!' ordered the princess.

The agent leaned on a huge lever and a giant walnut shell rolled over their heads along a bamboo stick cut in two lengthwise – similar to those in Arthur's water pipeline.

The walnut thundered past and wound up wedged in a hole in an apparatus that looked so complex that it was impossible, at first glance, to understand what it was for.

The agent opened a door in the walnut, like you would in a cable car. Our three heroes ducked inside and Arthur saw that the walnut was hollow, except for a part that had been formed into a bench.

Selenia pulled on a membrane in the middle of the walnut and attached it around herself like a seatbelt. Arthur watched her carefully and copied what she did rather than annoy her with the thousands of questions he was dying to ask.

'Bon voyage!' said the agent, slamming the door behind them.

Chapter 13

Another door, not too far away, opened slowly.

Grandma peeked into Arthur's room and saw that the boy was still sleeping, buried under the covers. All the better. She would be able to surprise him. She pushed the door open with her foot and entered carrying a magnificent pearly tray, which held a sumptuous breakfast.

She placed the tray down on the end of the bed.

'Breakfast is served!' Grandma announced with a satisfied smile. She tapped on the covers and opened the curtains. The bright morning light entered the room and illuminated the breakfast on the tray.

'Come on, you big good-for-nothing, it's time to get up!' she said, tugging back the covers.

Suddenly, she let out a shriek. Her grandson had been transformed into a dog!

Of course, it turned out to be just Alfred, who had slept in Arthur's bed. The dog wagged his tail, thrilled with his grand joke. Grandma, however, was less amused.

'ARTHUR!' she yelled.

The missing boy was in no danger of hearing her from inside his walnut. He was much too busy trying to figure out his seat belt.

Betameche pulled out a small white ball, as light as a dandelion. He shook it energetically and it lit up. Betameche released this pretty lamp and it floated in space, gently illuminating the cabin.

'I only have a white one. I'm sorry,' he said.

Arthur didn't mind. He was fascinated by the magic of this adventure. Even in his wildest dreams, he would never have imagined all this.

The transport agent took up the operator's position, a job as complicated as running an ocean liner. He pushed the first lever. A small needle turned on a disc, which listed the names of the seven lands that make up the Minimoys' world. The needle descended towards the dark part of the disc and stopped on FORBIDDEN LANDS. The enormous machine began to shake and the walnut slowly wobbled into place.

Arthur tried to see what was going on through the cracks in the walnut.

'I still don't understand how we are going to travel,' he said.

'Well – in the walnut,' responded Betameche, as if it were obvious. 'How else would we go?'

The little prince unfolded a map showing the seven lands.

'We are here. And we are going there!' Betameche pointed, as if it were a trip to the suburbs.

Arthur bent over the map and tried to figure out, despite the scale, where they were. He noticed that Necropolis was located not far from the house.

'I recognize that!' the boy said suddenly. 'Necropolis must be right under the garage and water tank.'

'What's a water tank?' asked Selenia, suddenly uneasy.

'It's where we keep all the water the house needs – in an enormous tank which it looks like is located here . . . just above Necropolis.'

Grandma turned on the fluorescent light in the garage. It was hopelessly empty. No trace of Arthur.

'Where did he go?' she asked the dog. Even if Alfred could speak, he knew very well that Grandma would never believe him.

'How many gallons does your tank hold, exactly?' questioned Selenia, obviously on the track of something.

'Oh, thousands upon thousands!' Arthur answered.

The face of the princess darkened. 'I think I'm starting to get a picture of his sinister plans,' she said.

'Whose?' Arthur asked.

'The plans of M.,' the princess replied, as if Arthur were thick-headed.

'Oh – Maltazard?' Arthur asked in a conspiratorial tone. Betameche and Selenia stiffened and he realized his mistake.

A muffled rumbling immediately arose from deep below them, signalling the approach of the kind of catastrophe that saying the name of M. always brought.

'In the name of a humpbacked gamoul!' screamed Selenia. 'Weren't you ever taught to watch your language?'

'I – I'm so sorry,' Arthur stammered, on the verge of panic.

The transport agent had his stethoscope placed against an enormous tunnel. He could feel the rumbling, and it was becoming louder.

'Departing for Necropolis in ten seconds,' he called, putting on his safety goggles.

Betameche pulled out two red, cottonwool-like balls from his pack. 'Do you want some mouf-moufs to put in your ears?' he asked Arthur.

'No, thanks,' replied the boy, his attention focused on the ground, which had started to vibrate.

'Are you sure? You're making a big mistake. These are top-quality mouf-moufs. They are completely new, never been used, and thanks to their self-cleaning fur, you can also –'

He was cut short mid-sentence by Selenia stuffing a mouf-mouf into his mouth.

The ground had been vibrating; now it was trembling furiously. Arthur had to hang on to keep from being flung all around.

The transport agent pushed a second lever. The needle turned once again around another disc. This one was the power indicator. The needle stopped in the red zone, where it read MAXIMUM.

Grandma was in a panic. She went through the house three times, and five times through the garden. She found not a trace of where Arthur might have gone. She stood one more time on top of the front steps and used her hands as a megaphone.

'ARTHUUUUR!'

Despite the noise and the shaking, Arthur perked up his ears. He could have sworn he'd heard a far-off voice calling his name. He leaned over to the tiny slit in the joint of the walnut and tried to locate the voice.

'Grandma?' he said.

'Blast off!' the conductor announced.

An umbrella opened automatically above the transport agent, while a veritable geyser shot out of the ground. Yes: the contraption holding the walnut was an automatic sprinkler. The force of the jet launched the walnut into the air and the trip was under way.

The nut hurtled through the air, crossing the garden at a height of several feet.

Through the slit, Arthur could see his grandma, who was turning to go back into the house.

'*Grandmaaaa*!' called the boy in one long shout.

Selenia was very sorry now that she had not put in her mouf-moufs.

Grandma turned around. Had she heard a small voice in the distance?

'Grandma! I'm here!' shouted Arthur, but his cry barely got through the walls of the walnut.

Grandma had neither seen nor heard anything. She stood watching the automatic sprinklers for a moment as they turned on, one after another.

Betameche finally managed to spit out his mouf-mouf.

'Selenia! Mouf-moufs are not meant to go in your mouth!' he yelped. 'That was a terrible thing to do. Now I'm thirsty!'

'I have a feeling you'll be wet enough soon, don't worry!' answered Selenia, who was trying to observe the water jet from a hole in the walnut.

'How long does the flight last?' asked Arthur, hanging on to the bench.

'A few seconds – if everything goes well,' the princess said in a concerned voice.

'What do you mean, if everything goes well?' said Arthur worriedly.

'If we don't have an unfortunate encounter with something!'

For once, Arthur felt that the princess was worried about nothing.

'What kind of unfortunate encounter could we have up here, in the middle of the air?' he asked with a grin.

'One like this!' she cried, curling up on the bench.

All of a sudden, an enormous bumblebee surged out of the beating rain of the sprinkler and smashed into the walnut. The shock was violent, like two cars crashing into each other. The walnut was knocked completely off course, while the bumblebee, its wings damaged, whirled in a tailspin towards the ground.

Inside the walnut, there was total panic and chaos. It was worse than an earthquake. The walnut crash-landed in a patch of tall grass, where it rolled for a moment, then came to a standstill.

Each of the passengers slowly came to. Beta noticed that his backpack was empty, its contents scattered.

'Now I have to repack the whole bag!' he sighed.

'I've told you a hundred times – you should carry

fewer things!' Selenia retorted, climbing to her feet.

Arthur was just happy to be alive and in one piece.

'Are trips around here always like that?' he asked.

'Long-distance trips like this are calmer than most of the ways we travel,' Selenia answered.

'Oh?' said Arthur, trying to imagine a less calm form of travel.

Selenia looked through the crack again.

'Let's wait for the rain to stop before we leave. We'll be able to see more clearly then.'

Grandma was still on the front steps when the automatic sprinklers shut off one by one. Silence was restored, magnifying her long sigh of desperation over her missing grandson.

She turned around, entered the empty house, and gently closed the door behind her.

'It's calmed down. We'll be able to go out now,' Selenia announced.

Betameche finished replacing things in his pack while his sister tried to open the door, which had been crushed during the accident.

'That awful bumblebee dented the door! It's stuck!'

Arthur tried to help her, to no avail.

Outside, a monstrous earthworm was approaching the walnut. It was not the nut that interested it but the appetizing dandelion leaves that the walnut had crushed during its landing.

The worm paused by the walnut and inadvertently gave it a shove so the whole thing rocked precariously.

'What was that?' Arthur worried.

'I don't know,' Selenia confessed. 'But we'd better not stay here.'

She unsheathed the magic sword and struck through the walnut shell with one swing. Unfortunately, she also pierced one of the segments of the earthworm outside, making it jump in surprise and hit against the walnut hard. The shot was powerful and precise. The walnut flew through the air. Of course, Betameche's backpack was flung open once again. As our three heroes clung to the walls, the shell rolled and rolled and finally plopped into the stream, where it was carried off like a small boat.

Arthur climbed to his feet, feeling seasick.

'Everything will be fine once we stop moving,' he managed nervously.

At that moment he noticed water starting to seep in through the joints in the shell and through the hole made by the sword. Selenia also saw what was happening and stared at the stream of water as if it were a poisonous snake.

'It's water! Arthur! We're taking in water!' she cried, starting to panic.

'It's terrible! We're doomed!' Betameche shrieked, clinging to his sister.

'Where are we? Arthur! Where are we?' demanded Selenia, now close to hysterics. Minimoys clearly reacted very badly to water.

'I don't know,' Arthur replied, pulling the sword out of her hands. He brandished the weapon over his head and struck a powerful blow along the joint. The walnut broke in two and each half split off to float separately, leaving Selenia and Betameche in one half, Arthur on the other.

'Arthur, do something! Help us!'

Arthur felt that this was somewhat unfair, as he was the one being carried away on the sinking half, and therefore should be the one calling for help. But chivalry has no limits.

'Don't worry, I'll save you!' called Arthur as the water climbed up to his waist. 'I know this stream. There's a curve up ahead on the right! I'll catch you there.'

'You call this a stream?' Selenia exclaimed, wondering whether Arthur was making fun of her.

'I'm coming!' Arthur called. He jumped into the water and tried, as best he could, to reach the bank.

'That boy is totally nuts!' Betameche observed, watching his friend swim.

Arthur managed to haul himself up onto the bank

and immediately disappeared into the tall grass.

Selenia and her brother hugged each other in terror.

'I don't want to die!' Betameche cried in a trembling voice.

'Everything will be all right – calm down!' Selenia replied, holding him close.

'Do you think he will abandon us?' asked her brother.

Selenia thought for a moment. 'I don't know human beings well enough to be sure, but based on the few that I've heard about – I'm afraid there's a good chance the answer is yes!'

'No!' cried the prince, devastated.

'Unless, of course . . . he's in love,' Selenia added, her tone of voice indicating that she thought this was an unlikely hypothesis.

Arthur ran until he was out of breath, jumping over branches, bending blades of grass, dodging insects. No obstacle could stop him, not even the colony of ants that he encountered along the way.

Betameche clung to the princess.

'Dear gods, make Arthur be in love with my sister! Please!'

Arthur ran like a maniac, as if his life depended on it.

There was no question about it: this young man was in love. He extricated himself from the miniature jungle and bolted out on top of the riverbank.

The walnut shell and its occupants appeared around a bend in the stream.

Betameche spotted Arthur.

'Selenia! He *is* in love!' he cried joyously.

'Let's not get carried away,' said the princess, a bit embarrassed.

Fortunately, Arthur heard none of this. He headed towards the stream, climbed on a tall stone, and leaped through the air. It was a world-class jump, worthy of a slow-motion replay on the evening news. As for the landing, it was not as smooth. Arthur smashed into the bottom of the walnut, knocking his friends over like bowling pins.

'You see! I didn't abandon you!' Arthur said proudly.

'Great! Instead of two of us dying, now it will be all three of us!' the princess retorted.

'No one is going to die, Selenia! You're not afraid of this little stream, are you?' Arthur wondered.

'But it's not a little stream, Arthur! It's a raging river and there, at the end of it, are the Devil's Falls!' the princess cried.

Arthur looked downstream. It did sound rather as if the noise were coming from the depths of the earth. Water sprayed all around them as the shell was tossed and spun.

'I – I didn't know that was coming!' Arthur stammered.

The falls roared louder and louder as they came into view. They were monstrous, and well deserved their name. They were so powerful they made Niagara Falls seem like a trickle.

Arthur was paralysed. The walnut, unfortunately, was not.

'Fabulous. Any bright ideas before we die?' Selenia asked, poking Arthur with her elbow.

Arthur gave a start. He looked around him thoughtfully and noticed a tree trunk that crossed the stream just before the falls.

'Do you have a rope in that three-hundred-function knife of yours?' he asked Betameche.

'Of course not! This is the small model,' the prince responded.

Arthur turned to Selenia. 'I have an idea! It's worth a try!' he said, jumping up. 'Can I have your belt?'

'He really is nuts!' said Betameche in amazement.

'I need your belt to make a rope so we can climb onto that tree trunk. It's our only chance.'

Selenia hesitated, then agreed. She removed her belt and handed it to him. Arthur picked up the magic sword and quickly tied the belt around the hilt.

'Beta first, then Selenia! We must be quick – we only have a few seconds!' Arthur announced, brandishing the sword.

'Do you have any idea what you're doing?' Selenia asked, crossing her arms.

'Sure – it can't be any more difficult than throwing a dart!' he answered, eyeing the tree. Arthur took aim and threw the sword with all his might. The blade shot through the air like a rocket and the sword planted itself in the middle of the tree.

'Yes!' Arthur cheered, waving his arms. 'Get ready, Beta!'

He had barely grabbed hold of the rope when Betameche was on his head, climbing like a monkey. Arthur balanced himself as best he could in the walnut as it tried to surge ahead down the river.

Betameche scaled the trunk and reached solid ground safely.

'Your turn, Selenia!' Arthur yelled over the deafening sound.

Selenia stared at the churning water below them in terror.

'Hurry up! I can't hold on much longer!' cried Arthur, who was using all his strength to hold her belt with two hands and the walnut with his feet. Selenia mustered her courage and clambered up the belt rope. At the top she stopped to catch her breath next to the sword, planted horizontally in the tree.

Arthur was nearly at the point of collapse. He let go of the walnut and it quickly floated away, leaving him hanging over the surging stream. The wind tossed him back and forth as he pulled himself painfully up the belt, hand over hand. The walnut shell flew over the edge and was swallowed up by the Devil's Falls, showing all too clearly what might have happened to Arthur and his companions.

Selenia climbed on the trunk and carefully descended to the ground. Arthur called on his last bit of energy and finally also reached the trunk of the tree.

Exhausted, he stayed there for a moment, kneeling, trying to catch his breath. Selenia had moved away. She was seated at the end of a branch, just above a small lake nearby, looking serene. Betameche was not far off, trying to squeeze out the bottom of his shirt. Arthur removed the sword from the tree and approached Selenia.

'Are you okay?' Arthur asked.

'I'd like my belt back,' she replied.

Arthur turned the sword and began to untie the knot.

'As for me, I have never been so scared in all my life!' Betameche admitted, delighted to have his feet back on solid ground.

Selenia shrugged her shoulders, as if to brush aside the adventure.

'It was no big deal. After all, it was only water!' she

said, with a lack of sincerity that was obvious to everyone.

As if in punishment, the heavens decided at that moment to cause her little branch to break, and the princess fell into the lake. 'Arthur! Help! I don't know how to swim,' she shrieked, flapping her arms.

Arthur ran out onto the branch and executed a magnificent dive, smacking headfirst, as it turned out, into the shallow mud of the lake. He stood up, holding his head. The water was only knee-deep. The princess was still struggling.

'Selenia, look! You can stand!'

Little by little, Selenia calmed down and realized that her feet could touch the bottom. She hesitated a moment, then stood up. The water just reached her calves.

'Didn't you say something about . . . it's only water?' Betameche reminded her mischievously.

'Can I have my belt now?' Selenia insisted, as angry as a hornet. She pulled it out of Arthur's hands and turned away to put it on.

'That's twice he's saved your life on the same day!' said Betameche, always ready to add fuel to the fire.

'He did what any gentleman would do in his place,' retorted the princess.

'Perhaps, but I think it's worth at least a brief word of thanks!' Betameche insisted.

Arthur signalled to him to let it drop. He wouldn't know how to react to a thank-you anyway. But Betameche loved to tease his sister about things that really annoyed her.

Selenia finished tying her belt and stalked up to a thoroughly intimidated Arthur. She stopped in front of her saviour and pulled the sword out of his hands.

'Thanks!' she said dryly, before passing in front of him and moving away.

Betameche smiled and shrugged. He could see that Arthur was more bewildered by the twists and turns of his sister's behaviour than he had been in the waters of the raging river. Beta grinned and shook his head at him.

'It's like that with princesses!'

Chapter 14

Grandma opened the front door to two policemen in uniform, holding their hats politely in their hands.

'Thank you for coming. I wasn't sure if you would get the message I sent with the postman. My husband disappeared four years ago and now my grandson . . . I can't take much more,' Grandma told them, twisting her lace handkerchief in her hands.

'Don't worry, Mrs S.,' Martin the policeman said, as kind as always. 'He has probably just run away. He must have been upset by everything that has been happening with Davido and the house and his parents – I'm sure he can't have gone too far.' He glanced at the horizon thoughtfully, not realizing that all he really needed to do was look down at the lawn.

'We will look for him, and I am sure that we will find him. You can count on us!' said the other policeman. For a moment, the two of them resembled the patrollers that Arthur had invented to travel up and down the trenches, as proud and brave as the heroes of a television series.

Grandma sighed, only partly comforted.

'Thank you, officers.'

The policemen went back to their car, replacing their hats on their heads.

Grandma waved goodbye as the police car left the garden. The vibration of the motor could be felt all through the ground and made the blades of grass tremble. At Minimoy level, this simple passage of a vehicle felt like an earthquake moving off into the distance.

'What was that?' asked Arthur in a worried voice.

'Humans,' responded Selenia, who was used to it.

'Oh?' mumbled Arthur, feeling a little guilty. He had never imagined the destruction that a human being could cause during the course of simple daily acts.

Betameche had unfolded his map, which was by now completely wet and washed out.

'We can't see anything! What are we going to do?' worried the little prince.

Arthur looked up towards the sky.

'Well, the sun is there, and the water tank is north. So we have to go in that direction!' he said, pointing to the road. 'Trust me!' he added with a new confidence.

He pushed aside three blades of grass and walked straight into a giant hole. Fortunately, he caught hold of a root as he slid by, narrowly avoiding a bone-crushing fall. He crawled back along the root and climbed up over the edge of the crater.

'What on earth is that?' he asked, mesmerized by the gaping hole.

'The humans, again,' Selenia replied sadly. 'Since yesterday it seems that they have sworn to kill us. They made dozens of holes like that all over the place.'

Aha – the holes dug by Arthur during his search for the treasure. He wanted to apologize, but he didn't quite have the courage to confess.

On the opposite side of the hole, an ant colony was building a road that descended to the bottom of the crater. Each ant carried a large sack of earth on its back.

'They have months of work ahead of them to repair and rebuild their system,' said Selenia.

'If only we knew why these idiots were digging holes everywhere!' Betameche added with great annoyance.

Arthur's heart sank to his boots. He wished he were brave enough to tell them that the idiot . . . was him.

'Don't be stupid, Beta! Humans don't know that we exist. So they can't possibly be aware of the damage they cause,' Selenia explained patiently.

'They will know soon enough,' Arthur interjected.

'And this type of catastrophe will never happen again. You have my word.'

'We'll see,' Selenia replied with natural scepticism. 'In the meantime, it is getting dark. We have to find a place to sleep.'

The orange light at the end of the day made the countryside seem almost monochromatic. Only the sky, awaiting the night, had kept its deep blue colour.

The little group headed towards a poppy, which waved proudly, very red and very alone. Betameche took out his multipurpose knife.

'Where did they put the metaglue?' he wondered, triggering the mechanism. He pushed a button and an enormous fireball shot out of the object. Arthur had just enough time to duck before the flames passed directly over his head.

'Oops!' said Betameche by way of an apology.

Selenia grabbed the knife from his hands.

'Give me that, or you're going to end up hurting someone!'

'I haven't had it very long. I got it as a birthday present,' explained the little prince to Arthur.

'How old are you?' Arthur asked.

'Three hundred and forty-seven years old. In eighteen years, I will be an adult,' explained Betameche happily.

Arthur took out a tangled-up abacus from Betameche's pack and tried to unravel this mystery.

Meanwhile, Selenia pushed the correct button and a spurt of metaglue attached itself to one of the poppy's petals. Spider-Man could not have done better.

She pulled a pick out from the knife and planted it in the ground. A small mechanism was released to wind the thread, pulling the petal down towards them and opening it, like the drawbridge of a fortress.

Arthur was still calculating.

'And . . . Selenia? How old is she?' he asked hesitantly.

'Pretty soon she'll be a thousand, the age of reason,' Betameche replied with a touch of envy. 'Her birthday is in two days.'

Arthur was beyond confusion. And he had been so proud to be ten years old!

The petal was now completely open and sufficiently lowered so that Selenia could climb into the flower. She took out her sword, caught the stamens, and cut them off at the base. Then she shook them until the little yellow balls fell off, forming a soft bed. Arthur watched her with awe.

Selenia threw away the stems of the stamens, now useless, and gestured to the two boys to climb into the flower. Betameche immediately threw himself down on the soft bed of yellow balls.

'I am dead tired! Good night!' he said, taking the time only to roll over before falling asleep.

Arthur was impressed. Here was somebody who didn't need Grandma's sleeping medicine.

'He falls asleep easily,' he commented.

'He is young,' Selenia explained.

'Three hundred and forty-seven years is still something!'

Selenia took the small luminous ball from her brother's backpack. She shook the ball to light it, and let it float inside the poppy.

'And you – will you really be a thousand in two days?'

'Yes,' the princess replied simply, cutting the metaglue thread with one stroke of her sword.

The petal immediately folded up and surrounded them.

Inside, the ambience was muffled and the light was soft. Selenia stretched out on the bed of yellow balls, like a cat relaxing on a carpet.

Arthur sat down beside her. Selenia was lost in her thoughts.

'In two days, I will succeed my father and rule over the Minimoy people until my own children are a thousand years old and succeed me in turn. That is how life is in the Seven Lands.'

Arthur remained quiet for a few moments. He was thoughtful.

'But . . . in order to have children, surely you have to have . . . a husband?'

'I know. But that's all right, I still have two days to find one! Good night!' she said, turning around.

Arthur felt like an idiot, full of questions. He leaned over to check, but she was already snoring. The boy sighed and stretched out next to the princess. He slipped his hands behind his head and let a smile travel across his face as he fell asleep.

It was almost night. The first stars were shining. There was only this luminous poppy in the middle of a sleeping forest, like a lighthouse on an invisible coast.

Beta's knife lay near him, shining in the moonlight, waiting for the morning.

But a hand appeared over the edge of the poppy petals and seized the knife. A rough hand . . . a terrifying hand. The night closed in and covered the criminal's escape.

Grandma went out onto the front steps, a candlelit lantern in her hand.

She searched the dark with the aid of this weak light, but everything around her was quiet and she saw no sign of Arthur.

Resigned, she hung the lamp on a hook over the front door and went back into the house, very unhappy.

The night passed, and the first rays of sunlight appeared, outlining the black hills on the horizon.

Chapter 15

The sun was also rising on the land of the Minimoys, and one of its rays had just peeked through the top of the poppy. Selenia awoke and stretched like a tiger. Then she jumped up and kicked each of the two boys.

'Everybody up! We have a long way to go!' Her cry echoed around the flower.

The two boys got up very slowly, still sleepy. Arthur ached all over from the events of the past few days. He knew they still had a long way to go before they got to Necropolis . . . and that if they didn't get there and back in time, his whole mission would be a failure.

Selenia pushed a petal with her foot and light invaded the flower. The two boys shielded their eyes from the strong sunshine.

'Okay! We have a new plan!' the princess declared.

Betameche slid down a petal to the ground. Arthur

followed him by jumping out. Selenia joined them, in turn, by sliding down the length of the petal, as if she were on a toboggan.

'Everyone to the showers!' she said, in her usual imperious voice.

Arthur stretched painfully.

'It's hard waking up in your country!' he complained. 'Where I live, my grandma brings me breakfast in bed every day.'

'Well, where we live, only the king is served in bed. And you're not king yet, as far as I know.'

Arthur turned a telltale shade of red. To be king was his secret dream – but not for the power or luxuries like breakfast in bed, but simply for the happiness of being married to the woman who soon would be queen. It didn't matter to him that she was a thousand years old.

'Don't complain!' Betameche said. 'She's been kicking *me* awake for the last two hundred years!'

Selenia stood under a dewdrop hanging at the tip of a blade of grass. She took one of her hairpins and pierced the drop neatly. A little stream of water spilled out. Selenia caught the water in her cupped hands and washed her face.

Arthur watched her do it with amusement. It was a change from his grandma's shower with its sticking curtain. He saw another drop, a bit larger, at the end of a leaf, and went over to stand underneath it.

'You shouldn't stand under that one,' the princess advised him.

'Oh? Why not?' asked Arthur.

'It's ripe,' she said, just as the drop detached itself and fell on Arthur. Instead of exploding, the drop absorbed him so he was trapped in the enormous mass like a fly in custard.

Betameche fell over laughing.

'You were fooled, just like a beginner!' he said.

'Help me, instead of laughing at me like a hyena! I'm trapped!' Arthur cried.

'I'm coming!' Betameche answered, bending his knees and jumping onto the drop, the way one would on a trampoline. Between bounces, he recited a little nursery rhyme that was very popular with the Minimoys:

'A little drop of water, that fell early in the day
Rolled up to the road to drown its sorrow.
No one heard it or helped it along the way.
So it left, saying "See you all tomorrow!"'

Selenia let him recite only two lines before pulling out her sword and slicing into the drop, causing it to explode. Betameche sprawled onto Arthur. The two boys were drenched – all showered for the day.

'I'm really hungry, aren't you?' Betameche said, as if nothing had happened.

'We'll eat later!' Selenia snapped, adjusting her sword and beginning to carve out their route through the grass. Betameche got up and began searching in his backpack for his knife.

'My knife is gone!' he said in a worried voice. 'Selenia, someone has stolen my knife!'

'Great news! That should keep you from hurting anyone!' his sister replied, already moving off into the undergrowth.

The little prince was angry, but he resigned himself to the loss and followed his companions.

Grandma appeared on the front steps of the house. The sun sent her its golden light, but no sign of Arthur.

The milk bottles weren't there, either. There was a note in their place. She picked it up and read.

Dear Madam,

Your account is overdue. We cannot continue to make deliveries until you have paid in full. Thank you.

Emile Johnson, director of the Davido Milk Corporation.

Grandma let out a brief laugh, as if the name on the evil note came as no surprise. She took down the hurricane lamp with its burned-out candle and went back into the house.

*

Betameche was wolfing down strange little red balls he'd picked off the leaves. Arthur picked one himself and looked at it sceptically.

'It's my favourite food!' the little prince said with his mouth full.

Arthur sniffed the rather transparent ball and bit into it. It was somewhat sweet, with a tart skin. It melted in the mouth like a super-light marshmallow. Arthur was immediately entranced and took another bite of the ball.

'It's terrific!' he admitted. 'What is it?'

'A dragonfly egg,' said Betameche.

Arthur froze, choked, and spat out everything, totally disgusted. Betameche roared with laughter and helped himself to another.

'Come and see!' Selenia cried from a clearing farther up ahead. Arthur ran to join her, brushing himself off as best he could.

Selenia was at the edge of a large canyon, clearly created by human hands.

All along the canal, someone had planted, vertically and at regular intervals, monstrous pipes with red and white stripes.

Arthur was mesmerized by this all-too-familiar horror . . . that he had created. It was, of course, his bamboo pole, marked at intervals with straws. Never had he imagined that this work, seen from below, could be so ugly.

'How terrible!' Betameche exclaimed. 'Humans are really horrible creatures!'

'Yes, seen from here, it's not very pretty,' Arthur admitted.

'Does anyone know what it's for?' Selenia asked.

Arthur felt obliged to provide an explanation. 'It's an irrigation system. It is used for transporting water.'

'Water? Again?' exclaimed Betameche. 'We're all going to end up drowning to death, aren't we?'

'I'm sorry. I didn't know,' said Arthur, extremely annoyed.

'Do you mean to say that *you* built this monstrosity?' asked the prince with a disgusted expression.

'Yes, I did, but it was meant to water the radishes!'

'Oh, you eat these disgusting things, too? Have I mentioned that humans are really mad?' Betameche said.

Selenia remained calm. She observed the construction analytically.

'Let us hope that your invention does not fall into the hands of M., because I can imagine how he might make use of it.'

Arthur stiffened – because of what she had said, but also because of what he saw behind Selenia's back.

'Too late,' said Betameche, who had seen the same thing.

Selenia turned and saw a group of henchmen

advancing from the bottom of the canyon. A few of them were riding mosquitoes; the others were on foot, cutting the straws to the ground with saws.

The cut straws fell to the ground and rolled towards the stream that had formed in the middle of the canyon. The straws then followed the path of the water, like enormous tree trunks travelling downriver.

Our heroes jumped into a bush and watched what was happening.

'I wonder what they are going to do with my straws,' Arthur said.

'As long as they get rid of them for us, it's okay by me!' Betameche replied.

Selenia hit him on the head.

'Think before speaking such foolishness! They know that Minimoys can't stand water, except for washing. And now they have a way to transport water . . . wherever they wish.' Her expression darkened, as if black thoughts were passing behind her eyes. 'And where do you think they are going to re-route the water?' she asked, knowing the answer already.

A henchman cut another straw that fell with a horrible crash.

'Towards our village?' Betameche realized. 'But that's horrible! We will all drown! All because of Arthur's invention?'

Arthur felt so guilty that he could hardly breathe.

He felt a large knot fill his stomach. He jumped up, angrily brushing away tears.

'Where are you going?' Selenia hissed.

'I'm going to make up for my stupidity!' he said with dignity. 'If what you say is true, the henchmen must be planning to send the straws straight to Necropolis – which means I'm going along with them!'

Arthur hurtled out of the grass and dashed into the end of the nearest freshly cut straw. Fortunately, the henchmen were too busy to notice him.

Arthur beckoned for his companions to accompany him.

'That boy is truly crazy!' Betameche announced.

'He's crazy, but he's right. The straws are going to end up in the forbidden city . . . and we will, too!' added Selenia before leaping out of her hiding place and throwing herself, in turn, inside the straw.

The henchmen had still seen nothing, but their work was bringing them steadily closer. Betameche sighed as he considered his choices.

'Okay, but they *could* ask me for *my* opinion from time to time, all the same!' he remarked in an offended tone before running to join his comrades.

The henchmen reached the straw occupied by our runaways and kicked it down to the stream. The straw slid onto the water and began to float away. Inside, our three heroes were thrown in all directions.

'I hate our means of transportation. My back is aching all over!' Betameche complained.

'Stop whining and give me your mouf-moufs!' his sister ordered.

'If it's to put them in my mouth, no way!'

'Give them to me!' the princess cried with authority.

Betameche grumbled, but he took the mouf-moufs out of his pack and handed them to his sister.

'We are going to plug up the holes,' Selenia explained throwing a ball to each end. 'Mints, quick!'

Beta grabbed his peashooter and inserted a small white candy. He blew the tube in the direction of the mouf-mouf, which inflated instantly, hardened, and turned violet.

He did the same thing on the other side, and now the straw was completely sealed on either end.

Selenia rubbed her hands happily.

'This way, we won't take on any water!'

'And we can travel calmly!' added Betameche, stretching himself out in the hollow of the straw.

The voyage did not remain calm for long, however. The little stream turned to merge with a stronger current of water that felt decidedly larger.

'Do you hear that muffled sound that keeps getting louder?' Betameche asked.

Selenia listened. There *was* a sound – a background

noise that resembled a very low vibration.

'Hey, Mr Know-It-All, do you know where this current is heading?' Selenia asked Arthur.

'Not exactly. But all the currents meet up with each other at some point, so they always end up at the same place, which is to say . . .'

Little by little, it dawned on Arthur what he was about to say.

'Devil's Falls!' our three heroes screamed in a single, panicked voice.

It was the end of the relaxed journey. The straws were rushing towards the fathomless waterfall.

'You always have such good ideas, don't you!' Selenia yelled at Arthur.

'I didn't think that –'

'Of course you didn't! Next time, *try* thinking before you act!' she screamed. 'Betameche, find something. We have to get out of here!'

'I'm moving as fast as I can!' replied the little prince, who was once again emptying his backpack of useless objects.

'I'm sure it'll be fine,' Arthur said. 'The moufmoufs are blocking the two ends. Nothing can happen to us! Besides, the falls are not that large – hardly three feet tall!'

The straw reached the edge of the monstrous waterfall, which was more like a thousand feet tall by

Minimoy measurements. The straw tipped over gently and plunged into the void.

'AIIIIEEEEEEEEEE!!!!' screamed our three heroes, but the deafening sound of the falls drowned out their voices.

After plunging for several seconds that seemed more like several hours, the straw landed with a splash among foaming whirlpools. The straw got stuck in a spin, came unstuck, rolled, and then, carried by the current, ended up heading towards a small, much calmer lake.

There was a pause.

'I really hate public transportation!' Betameche complained.

'We are past the falls. It will be calmer now!' Arthur assured them, untangling himself from Betameche's things.

The straws dispersed in the middle of the lake. It was almost too calm to be true.

Suddenly, a creature with jointed feet landed on top of their straw, like a car falling from the sky. Through the semi-transparent wall of the straw, they could see the outline of its feet. And, given their unfamiliar shape, there was cause for some concern.

'What is that?' asked Betameche, frozen with terror at the bottom of the straw.

'How should I know?' Selenia replied edgily.

'Quiet!' whispered Arthur. 'If we are quiet it will surely continue on its way.'

Arthur appeared to be right – for about three seconds. Then a monstrous saw sliced into the straw, a hair's breadth away from Selenia, who screamed.

Horror reigned. Splinters flew everywhere and the noise was unbearable. The top of the straw was cut off, level with the small accordion section where a straw bends.

All three tried to scramble on all fours to the opposite end, but the creature leaped forward, blocking their way. Our heroes found themselves in the accordion section, on the water's edge, facing their doom.

The creature sawed again, level with the other end of the accordion. It detached the small, bulging section of straw hiding our three friends. This seemed to be the only part in which it was interested.

The three of them were terrified and clung to each other for comfort.

The creature was still standing on the striped accordion section. Only the bottom of its feet could be seen. But something must have caught its attention, because now the imprint of its knees, and then its hands, appeared. It was on all fours above them. Its head appeared, upside down, at the opening of the straw.

The creature had long braids, decorated with seashells, which hung loose in the air.

It was a Koolomassai. The creature lifted his safety goggles, observed our terrorized heroes for a moment, and smiled a wide smile, showing beautiful white teeth. Since his head was upside down, his smile was, too, and Arthur was not sure what to think.

'What are you doing in there?' asked the Koolomassai, laughing.

Selenia spotted a mosquito approaching in the distance.

'If the henchmen find us, we will not have the pleasure of telling you!' she snapped humourlessly.

The Koolomassai got the message and stood up.

'Is there a problem?' asked the henchman, landing his mosquito next to what remained of the straw. Arthur, Betameche and Selenia held their breaths, huddled just out of the henchman's sight.

'No, nothing special. I was just checking to see if this was damaged,' answered the Koolomassai employee nonchalantly.

'We are only interested in the tubes. This part doesn't interest us,' said the henchman, pointing to the accordion section.

'What luck! This is exactly the part that interests *us*! I guess we won't have anything to argue about, then!' added the worker cheerfully.

But the henchmen, as a general rule, did not appreciate humour.

'Hurry up. The master is waiting,' barked the henchman, whose patience and intelligence seemed equally limited.

'No problem!' answered the Koolomassai. 'Don't move,' he whispered to Arthur and the others. 'I'll come back for you!'

Then he disappeared, jumping from one straw to another.

'Hurry up, the master is waiting!' cried the Koolomassai to his comrades, who were dispersed among the other straws floating on the lake. The workers half-heartedly sped up, but with little enthusiasm. (It was a bit like those taxi drivers who deliberately slow down when you are in a hurry.)

The Koolomassai used a long stick to guide the straws towards another current of water. In passing, he separated the accordion sections and pushed them towards the shore. Our three friends followed the Koolomassai's advice and didn't move.

A kind of crane, built from wood and vines, caught the little piece of straw with our adventurers inside and tossed it into an enormous basket. The accordion section landed among a veritable harvest of twenty others.

The basket was attached to the back of an enormous insect – a gamoul, which is an extremely strong type of beetle that often served as a mule. The animal was also used in many popular expressions, such as 'stubborn as a gamoul' or (and this was the case here) 'loaded down like a gamoul'.

'Where are we?' Arthur asked uncertainly.

'On the back of a gamoul. The Koolomassai is hiding us for the moment,' Selenia said.

'He is hiding us so that he can betray us!' said Betameche.

'If he wanted to betray us, he would have done so already!' Selenia replied sensibly. 'I'll bet we are going to a safe place now.'

Chapter 16

A metallic trapdoor rolled open in the side of the hill. The gamoul rose up onto its legs and prepared to empty the contents of the basket into a black hole that bore a strange resemblance to a garbage chute.

'This is your safe place?' asked Betameche anxiously.

Dozens of accordion sections slid down into the black hole in an impressively chaotic manner, rolling to a standstill several inches below, on the dark ground. Arthur, Betameche and Selenia managed to stay in their straw.

Nothing moved. Silence returned. The three heroes glanced at one another uncertainly.

'He said not to move. So we don't move until he comes to get us!' said Selenia authoritatively.

An automatic arm swooped up the accordion section and placed it vertically, standing on end, squishing the three of them into a heap at the bottom. The piece of straw began moving along a conveyor belt. The mechanical arm continued to do its work, aligning all of the accordion sections on the belt that carried them away.

A little farther down, another machine embedded a luminous ball in the centre of each accordion, like an internal crown. Our heroes just managed to avoid getting 'crowned' themselves.

The accordion section of the straw now had an orange light in its centre, and they began to understand how these objects would be put to use.

A final machine caught the section of straws and attached them to a cable that stretched into space, a magnificent garland hung with evenly spaced striped Chinese lanterns. The lights continued around the edge of a circular dance floor. It was, in fact, an old record, placed on an antique record player that served as both bar and dance floor underground. The warm light from the lanterns created a muted ambience for meeting people. There were also lots of small tables provided for this purpose. Towards the right side were the arm and stylus of the record player and the DJ. Towards the left, the enormous bar was buzzing with activity. Half the customers were obviously henchmen from the royal army of M.

Arthur and his friends observed this strange nightclub from above, still gripping the inside of their 'Chinese lantern'.

'I can't hold on much longer,' said Arthur, exhausted.

'Do you really want to go down there?' asked Selenia, pointing with her nose towards a new group of henchmen that had just entered the bar.

After a moment's thought, Arthur replied, 'I guess I can hold on a little longer!'

Just then they saw their Koolomassai friend arrive on the dance floor. He was followed by his boss, who was taller and broader.

Their Koolomassai looked up and examined the lanterns one by one, searching for the fugitives. Since the lanterns were translucent, they were rather easy to spot, especially since they were clinging to the sides in rather contorted positions.

'It's okay! You can jump down!' their Koolomassai called to them with a smile.

Arthur was so exhausted he immediately fell to the dance floor. He got up, somewhat embarrassed, and Selenia fell right into his arms, followed by Betameche, who fell into his sister's arms. Arthur remained like that for a moment, with these two parcels in his arms. Then his knees collapsed, and the three tumbled to the ground.

'These are the three that the henchmen are looking

for everywhere?' the bigger guy asked, somewhat sceptically.

'I thought so – but I might have been a little excited from all the candyfruit,' the Koolomassai confessed.

'You know, it's the root you're supposed to eat, not the entire tree!'

'Oh – really?' the employee replied.

'Yes!' said the boss. 'Go on, get out of here. I'll take care of them.'

Their Koolomassai moved away, looking dubious, while our three heroes got to their feet. All of a sudden, the boss's face changed, putting on a smile worthy of a used-car salesman.

'My friends!' he announced, with arms open wide and teeth showing. 'Welcome to the Jaimabar Club!'

A rickety-looking mosquito put four glasses down on the table next to them.

'Would you all like some jack-fire? It's the special drink of the house for our guests who aren't old enough to have alcohol!' explained the boss.

'Oh, yes! cried Betameche enthusiastically.

'Jack?' the boss said, rapping on the mosquito's head. 'Hit it!'

The mosquito sprayed the red liquid directly into the glasses. It foamed, smoked, and ended by bursting into flames.

The boss blew on the flame until it was just smoke.

'Long life to the Seven Lands!' he proclaimed, extending his glass for a toast.

The others each extinguished the flames in their drinks and lifted their glasses. The boss drank his down in one gulp, followed immediately by Selenia and Betameche. Arthur didn't move. Wisely, he first wanted to see the effect of the drink.

'That's great!' said Betameche.

'It's very thirst-quenching,' Selenia added.

'It is my children's favourite drink!' the boss said proudly.

The three faces turned towards Arthur, who still hadn't drunk any. It was almost humiliating.

'To the Seven Lands!' cried the boy, against his better judgement.

He raised his glass and drank it down in one gulp, which was a big mistake. He turned red as a beetroot. It was as if he had just consumed a raw jalapeño in chilli sauce and maple syrup. It was as if he had swallowed a volcano. Arthur felt sure smoke must be coming out of his ears, as if he had just spent twelve hours in a sauna.

'Yes . . . thirst-quenching!' he squawked, with what little remained of his voice.

Betamache ran his finger around the bottom of the glass and licked it.

'It has a slight taste of apple!' said the young connoisseur.

'It's not the least bit like apple!' Arthur replied.

A group of henchmen appeared in the doorway, surveying the place, as if they were searching for something or someone. Selenia ducked her head to hide her face.

'Nothing to be afraid of!' the boss assured them. 'Those are just recruiters. They take advantage of the weakness of certain customers to make them enlist in the royal army. As long as you are with me, you have nothing to worry about.'

Our friends relaxed.

'How is it that the henchmen have not yet alienated or oppressed your people, the way they have all the others who live in the Seven Lands?' Selenia asked suspiciously.

'Oh, that's simple!' said the boss. 'We produce ninety per cent of the candyfruit root they love so much. The army of henchmen wouldn't last a day without their root! Since we are the only ones that can prepare it, they leave us alone.'

Selenia was a bit sceptical about this whole business.

'What plant do these roots come from?'

'That depends. Linden, chamomile, verbena –only what's natural!' he affirmed with a sly smile. 'Would you like to try some?' he offered, like a snake suggesting an apple.

'No, thank you, Mr . . .?'

'My friends call me Max,' the boss replied with a smile showing all thirty-eight teeth. 'And you? What is your name?'

'I am Selenia, daughter of King Sifrat de Matradoy, fifteenth of that name, ruler of the First Lands.'

'Wow!' said the boss, acting impressed. 'Your highness!' he added, bending over to kiss her hand. Selenia pulled it away to point to her companions.

'This is my brother, Saimono de Matradoy de Betameche. You can call him Beta.'

Arthur had recovered enough to introduce himself.

'And I am Arthur! From the house of Arthur! Why have you cut all my straws?' he asked. The jack-fire was making his head spin and he was having trouble forming coherent thoughts.

'It's a business arrangement. The henchmen asked us to clean them and guide them to the black river, the one that leads directly to Necropolis.'

At this piece of news, our three heroes sat up, full of hope.

'That is precisely where we need to go! Can you help us?' the princess asked.

'What? Slow down, Princess! Necropolis is a one-way trip! Why would you want to go to such a place?' inquired the boss.

'We have to destroy M. before he destroys us,' Selenia answered.

'Oh, is that all?' Max said sarcastically.

'That is all,' Selenia replied, as serious as ever.

Max looked worried. 'Why does M. want to destroy you?' he asked.

'It's a long story,' the princess assured him. 'Let's just say that in one more day I have to choose a husband and succeed my father, and M. the cursed does not want this to happen. He knows that once I have assumed power, he may never be able to invade our land. It is written in the prophecy.'

Max seemed very interested, especially by the part concerning the husband.

'Marriage, eh? What is the name of the lucky man?'

'I don't know. I haven't chosen him yet,' replied the princess.

Max sensed an opportunity. 'Before we continue, you deserve a little fun! Jack, bring us some more of that excellent drink! This one's on me again!' offered the boss, to Beta's great delight.

While Jack the mosquito busied himself with refilling the glasses, Max scurried over to the DJ, located next to the arm of the record player.

'Easylow! Spin this platter for me!' the boss told him hurriedly.

DJ Easylow leaned over to the back of the record player and woke up the two Koolomassai who were slumped there asleep on their hoards of candyfruit root.

'Get up, guys! Time to work!' Easylow told them.

The two sleepers slowly got up and stretched, as if they were made of marshmallow. They walked over to an enormous five-volt battery and rolled it up to the battery receptacle. As soon as the battery was engaged, the lights went on over the dance floor. The turntable began to move and Easylow pushed the stylus to the song of his choice.

Max leaned over to Selenia.

'May I have this dance?' he asked, with exaggerated politeness.

Selenia smiled. Arthur did not. 'We have a long road to travel, Selenia! We should be going!' he said, very worried about this new competition.

'Five minutes of relaxation never hurt anyone!' Selenia replied, accepting Max's offer as much for the fun of dancing as for the opportunity to tease Arthur.

Max and Selenia stepped onto the dance floor and started to waltz.

'Beta! Do something!' Arthur cried.

Betameche, in response, drank down his jack-fire.

'What do you want me to do?' he asked. 'She will be a thousand years old soon. She can make her own decisions!'

Arthur scowled. Betameche glanced from the dance floor to the bar and noticed a Koolomassai with a knife in his belt.

'Hey, that's my knife!' Betameche exclaimed. 'I'm going to have a word or two with that thief!' The little prince got up, gulped down his sister's jack-fire, and headed towards the bar with a determined step.

Arthur was alone, desperate, at his wits' end. He grabbed his glass and gulped down its contents. Perhaps the magical jack-fire would make him so confused that things would start to make sense again.

Chapter 17

It was like a game: Max kept trying to get closer to Selenia, and she politely resisted, glancing over at Arthur whenever she could to see how he was reacting.

'You know, finding a husband in such a short time won't be easy!' Max observed. 'But I can help you out, if you like.'

'That's very nice of you, but I think I can manage,' Selenia replied, amused.

'I like to be of service. It's my nature. Besides, you are in luck; things are rather calm at the moment. I have only five wives right now!'

'Five wives? That must be a lot of work, keeping them happy!' Selenia said with a smile.

'I'm a very hard worker!' Max assured her. 'I can work day and night, seven days a week, without ever getting tired!'

Arthur was slumped on the table, his sad eyes following the sight of his beloved princess dancing with someone else.

'Anyway, she's too old for me!' he said to himself. 'A thousand years old, although she looks my age. I'm only ten!'

A henchman recruiter sat down opposite him, blocking his view of the princess.

'What's a handsome fellow like you doing in a place like this?' the henchman asked, with the smile of a hunter who has just smelled a pigeon.

Betameche reached the bar and shoved the knife thief, who splashed his drink all over himself.

'Hey! Watch it!' said the Koolomassai in an extremely annoyed tone of voice.

'That's my knife! You stole it from me!' Beta yelled, as belligerent as a pit bull. 'It's *my* knife. I got it for my birthday!'

The Koolomassai reached out his arm and held the boy at a distance.

'What? Calm down, grumpy! What if it just so happens that I have the same knife as you do?'

'It's mine, I'm sure of it! I could pick it out of a thousand! Give it to me!' insisted Betameche.

A henchman approached the two of them with the confident stride of an officer.

'Is there a problem?' asked the soldier.

'No! Everything is fine!' the Koolomassai assured him in honeyed tones.

'No! Everything is *not* fine!' Betameche retorted. 'He stole my knife!'

The thief began to smile, as if it were all a joke.

'He's just fooling around! I can explain everything, Captain!' As if by magic, the Koolomassai pulled out two slices of candyfruit root with a smug air.

'Would you like a little root?' suggested the sly devil.

The henchman hesitated, but couldn't resist for long. He lifted up his visor and revealed his face. This was the first time Betameche had seen the face of a henchman, since they were usually helmeted, and he immediately realized he could have happily gone through life without it. The henchman's head was completely bare – of everything. No hair, no eyebrows, no ears, no lips. The face was almost round and smooth, like a stone polished by years of erosion. It was a multicoloured insect face, eaten away by diseases. The two small red eyes were empty, like eyes that have seen too much war. In short, he was not pleasant to look at. The henchman took the root and put it in his mouth, which was barely a hole in his face. He chewed for a minute, then smiled a frightening smile.

Betameche was worried. Things did not seem to be going his way, to say the least. How had they got themselves into this mess?

*

Meanwhile, Max was still working on Selenia.

'So? What do you say?' he asked.

'Well, you're very nice, but marriage is an important choice that cannot be decided too quickly,' Selenia replied, as playful as a cat with a mouse.

She cast a glance at Arthur, but he was not looking at her. He had his nose in a contract that he was moments away from signing. The henchman recruiter was handing him a pen and sliding the contract towards him. Arthur bent over to sign, but Selenia's hand appeared and prevented him from doing so.

'Excuse me, officer, but I would like to dance with this boy one last time before he commits himself to something other than me!'

The henchman didn't like this, but Selenia was already dragging Arthur onto the dance floor.

'It's very nice of you to give me this dance!' Arthur said to her, with a happy smile.

'The jack-fire is really having a peculiar effect on you, you idiot. Do you know what you were about to sign?' Selenia asked him with immense irritation.

'No. Not really, but it's not important!' Arthur answered.

'Do you really think I will marry a guy who gets woozy after a little jack-fire and who dances with two left feet?'

It took Arthur a few seconds, but he got the message. He stood up straighter and attempted to control his feet better. Selenia smiled at the superhuman efforts of her companion, who was doing what he could to fight the effects of the magic jack-fire.

'That's better,' she conceded.

Easylow watched the couple from a distance.

'Are you going to let that dwarf steal her away from you?' he asked Max, who was standing next to him, also watching them.

'A little competition never did anyone any harm!' Max said with a smile, not really worried.

Arthur was reviving a little. Dancing was clearing his head. He took a chance. 'Do you – do you really think that . . . I might have a chance with you? Despite, you know . . . our age difference?'

Selenia started to laugh.

'In our country, we count years according to the flowering of the selenielle, the royal flower – that's where my name comes from, too.'

'Oh! Well, then . . . in Minimoy years, how old am I?'

'About a thousand years. Like me,' replied the princess, amused.

Arthur puffed out his chest a little, flattered by his sudden maturity. It made him want to ask a million questions.

'And were you ever a little girl like me? I mean – I'm a boy, of course – but were you . . . a little girl like the ones in my neighbourhood? My size?'

'No. I was born a Minimoy,' answered Selenia, who was somewhat disturbed by the question. 'And I have never travelled beyond the Seven Lands.'

There was regret in the voice of the princess, but she would never admit it.

'I would like to take you, one day . . . into my world,' Arthur confided, already saddened by the idea of ever having to leave her, even if it was in a thousand years.

Selenia was increasingly ill at ease.

'Sure, why not!' she replied, somewhat disdainfully, as if to minimize the importance of their words. 'But while we are waiting, may I remind you that we have a mission to complete. Remember Necropolis?'

The word resounded in Arthur's head and woke him up instantly.

The henchman recruiter knew he had lost his client and he returned to the bar, looking for a new victim. He passed by Betameche, still engaged in conversation with the thief and the officer. The Koolomassai thief was in fine form, talking his smoothest talk.

'And then, suddenly, I tripped on a knife stuck in the ground! First I thought it was a trap, you know?'

The henchman laughed, his mouth full of root. 'That's a good one!' he guffawed, without knowing himself whether he was referring to the joke or to the candyfruit.

Betameche sighed in desperation. He did not seem destined to recover the knife that the henchman officer was now slowly turning in his hands.

The recruiting agent joyfully seized two new victims and dragged them off. Selenia watched them leave. It gave her an idea.

'I bet that if we follow those recruiting agents, at least two of us can reach Necropolis!'

Arthur agreed.

'You are right! At least two of us will get there! It is our mission!' he cried, carried away by a burst of excitement. 'Once we are there, I will find my grandfather, I will discover the treasure, and I will give that cursed Maltazard a thrashing that he will never forget!'

The whole world came to a halt. Easylow grabbed the edge of the disc and stopped the music. Twenty henchmen turned to see what joker had had the bright idea of pronouncing this forbidden name.

'Oops!' said Arthur timidly, realizing his mistake.

'I don't know if you would make a good prince, but in the meantime, you are truly the king of blunderers!' Selenia said reproachfully.

Max began to grin. 'Things are picking up here,' he rejoiced. 'Showtime!'

He signalled to Easylow, who released the disc and kicked the stylus. The music started up again.

The henchmen were closing in on the retreating couple. Things were looking very, very bad.

'Arthur? You have three seconds to clear your head of the jack-fire!' Selenia barked.

'What? Okay! But . . . what can I do to get clear in three seconds?'

Selenia smacked him right in the face – the kind of slap you don't want to get very often. Arthur shook his head. His teeth felt like they were floating.

'Thanks. I'm better now!'

'You should be!' she said, drawing the magic sword.

'And what am I supposed to fight with?' worried Arthur.

'You figure it out!'

Selenia was on her guard, as the disc, which continued to turn, brought them near Max and his DJ.

'Hey, kid!'

The boss had pulled out a sword and he threw it to Arthur.

'Thank you, sir!' replied the boy, amazed by this chivalry.

'Go ahead! Make them all dance for me!' said Max to his DJ, who pushed the stylus into a new groove. Arthur took his position alongside Selenia, while the henchmen deployed themselves in a circle around the pair.

Betameche had followed the henchman officer who was holding his knife and helpfully advised him. 'If you press number seventy-five, you will have a laser sabre. It's a classic but always effective.'

'Oh? Really? Thanks, kid!' the henchman replied, still on a woozy sugar high from the candyfruit root. He pressed number seventy-five and immediately a monstrous flame set fire to his helmet and everything inside it. The henchman's body had not moved, but his head was now in ashes.

Betameche recovered his knife from the henchman's hands.

'A thousand pardons. My mistake. Maybe it's the opposite? Fifty-seven?'

Betameche pressed button fifty-seven and the knife released a laser sabre, blue like steel.

'That's better!'

The three heroes were united once again, but things did not look good. They stood back-to-back, swords in front of them, forming a dangerous triangle.

All at once, the henchmen let out their famous battle cry, and the fighting began.

Easylow put on his cut-off gloves, grabbed the edge of the disc, and began to scratch to give the battle some rhythm.

Selenia executed pass after pass, demonstrating her skill and agility. She had the grace and power of a true knight.

Betameche had an easier weapon and caused plenty of damage, sweeping his sabre in wide arcs and knocking over henchmen as if he were bowling.

Arthur had less experience, but he was lively enough to fend off blows. He swung out his sword to repel an assault, but the attacker smashed his weapon to smithereens.

Max pretended to be disappointed. 'Oh, poor boy! Who could have given him such a poor-quality sword?' he said with false compassion. Easylow looked at him, and the two mercenaries began to laugh like hyenas.

Arthur ran around the dance floor, dodging the blows raining down from every side. He took refuge on the other side of the stylus. The henchmen scrambled to get to him but wound up crashing into the rapidly moving needle, causing it to skip and scratch out the music like they do in the best dance clubs.

'That kid has rhythm in his blood!' observed Max with a professional grin.

Three henchmen stood in front of Betameche, all also armed with laser sabres.

'Three against one?' Betameche scoffed. 'Have you no shame? Very well, I triple the power!'

Betameche pressed a button that made his laser disappear and replaced it with a bouquet of flowers.

'Um . . . beautiful, aren't they?' he joked, embarrassed by his mistake.

The henchmen yelled and charged towards the little prince, who took off running. He threw himself under a table, where he found Arthur already hiding.

'My weapon isn't working any more!' exclaimed Betameche, searching for the right button.

'Mine isn't, either!' Arthur replied, showing him the broken-off blade.

A henchman approached the table and sliced it in half with a single blow from his laser sabre. The two friends rolled to either side.

'On the other hand, his works very well!' cried Arthur with great alarm.

Betameche started punching buttons at random on his knife and ended up releasing a weapon of sorts: a minuscule pipe that shoots out one hundred soap bubbles per second. A cloud quickly formed around them – not really dangerous to anyone but very practical for hiding.

The henchmen rapidly lost track of their targets. This made them extremely angry, and they beat the air with their swords, succeeding only in bursting several pretty, multicoloured soap bubbles.

Selenia eliminated one henchman, then ducked to

her knees, sword over her head, to block the assault of another warrior. She unsheathed the backup knife that the henchman had strapped to his ankle and planted it in his foot. The henchman was paralysed with pain.

'Hey, careful over there! Don't damage my floor!' the boss called angrily.

Arthur crawled out from under the cloud of bubbles and tripped over Beta's backpack. He found himself sprawled across the feet of a henchman. The warrior slowly raised his sword, savouring the evil moment.

Arthur was doomed. He tried to scramble away and felt his hand close over some mysterious pellets that had fallen out of the backpack. With a yell, he threw them at the henchman's feet, without the slightest idea of what might happen. It could save him or blow him up before the henchman got to him. Either way, he had nothing to lose.

The little glass balls scattered around the feet of the henchman, who stopped to peer at them, too stupid not to be curious.

A magnificent bouquet of exotic flowers suddenly blossomed out of the floor, as if by magic. It was bigger than the henchman!

'Flowers! Isn't that nice!' said the henchman. He stepped around the bouquet and approached Arthur menacingly. 'I'll place them on your grave!' the warrior snarled, brandishing his sword.

He was blinded by his own evil, and so he failed to see, behind him, the gigantic flower opening its vast, carnivorous mouth. The beautiful plant clamped the henchman in its jaws, then took the time to chew him very carefully. Arthur watched, stupefied, as the monstrous flower opened its mouth and emitted a loud burp.

'Excuse *you*!' said Arthur, a bit disgusted.

Betameche pushed another button on his knife. This *had* to be the right one. There were three henchmen around him who did not look in the mood for games.

A three-beamed laser appeared from the knife.

Betameche grinned and proudly flourished his weapon. The three henchmen looked at one another, then each one of them pressed a button on his laser, releasing a new sabre with six rotating blades. Betameche was petrified.

'Wow – is that a new model?' he asked, trying to distract them.

The henchman facing him nodded with an evil grimace, then struck the prince such a violent blow that his knife was sent flying. The lasers retracted and the knife slid across the ground to where a foot reached out and stopped it. A foot wearing a warrior henchman's boot, size forty-eight . . . covered with blood.

Easylow grabbed the disc and stopped the music. The dance floor froze. The fighting paused. Silence greeted the leader of the henchmen: Darkos, Prince of Shadows – son of Maltazard.

Our three heroes came together, gasping with exhaustion.

Darkos had the appearance of a henchman, but his build was more imposing and his armour more frightening. He was better armed than a fighter plane; in all the Seven Lands, there did not exist a weapon that he did not possess. Except, perhaps, for this little knife that he had blocked with his foot. He bent down slowly and picked up the object.

'So, Max – having a party and not inviting your friends?' he said ominously, turning the knife over in his hands.

'Nothing official!' Max assured him, smiling to hide his unease. 'This was just a small, improvised party to welcome the new clientele!'

'New clientele?' Darkos mused. 'Show me.'

The warriors parted to each side of the dance floor, revealing our three heroes standing together.

As he approached them, Darkos saw the princess, and a big smile of recognition spread across his face.

'Princess Selenia? What a pleasant surprise!' he said, stopping directly in front of her. 'What is someone of your rank doing in a place like this at such a late hour?'

'We came for a little dancing,' she replied defiantly. Darkos took the bait.

'Very well – then let's dance!' he said, snapping his fingers.

A henchman hit the record-player arm, landing the needle on a slow dance. Darkos bowed slightly and offered the princess his arm.

'I would rather die than dance with you, Darkos,' Selenia snapped.

The atmosphere felt as if a button had just been pushed to launch an atomic bomb. The henchmen edged away worriedly. Violence and destruction always resulted when Darkos was insulted, especially in front of everyone. He stood up slowly from his bow, and smiled a sinister smile.

'Your wish is my command!' he said, unsheathing his enormous sword. 'You will dance alone for eternity!'

Darkos raised his weapon, ready to cut Selenia into pieces.

'What about your father?' the princess said calmly. The creature stopped his arm in midair. 'That's right, Darkos – what will your father, M. the cursed, say when you tell him that you have killed the princess he's been searching for? The only person who can bring him the ultimate power that he so dreams of having?'

Selenia had hit the right note. Junior was clearly thinking carefully now.

'Do you think he'll congratulate you? Or that he'll have you burned with the tears of death, like he burned all his other sons?'

There was uneasiness in the ranks. Selenia had mastered her subject and Darkos slowly lowered his weapon.

'You are right, Princess. I thank you for your clairvoyance,' he said, replacing his sword in its sheath. 'It is true that dead, you have no value. But alive . . .!' He smiled the smile of someone who has had a very wicked idea.

But Max had read his thoughts. 'Easylow – it's closing time!'

The DJ winked and headed towards the back of the room.

'Take them away!' Darkos cried, and thirty henchmen rushed towards our heroes.

Arthur watched the attackers approach, like a surfer watching a tidal wave.

'We're going to need a miracle!' said Arthur.

'Death is nothing if the cause is just!' cried Selenia, ready to die nobly, as befits a princess. She brandished her sword in front of her and screamed a battle cry to give herself courage.

At that exact moment, the lights went out. Whether it was Selenia's scream, or DJ Easylow cutting off the power in the back, it was now completely dark, and there was total panic. Sounds of iron, boots, blades and chattering teeth rang out.

'Gotcha!'

'There they are!'

'I have one!'

'Let me go, you imbecile!'

'Sorry, boss!'

'Ouch! Who bit me?'

This is just a sample of the sounds rising from the shambles once they were plunged into darkness.

Finally a match flared, illuminating Max's laughing face. He lit a lamp and surveyed the amusing spectacle. Darkos came and stood in the circle of light. He was mad with fury and the red light did nothing to help his looks.

'What is going on here?' he spluttered with rage.

'It's ten o'clock. Closing time,' Max responded cheerfully.

'You close at ten o'clock now?' growled Darkos.

'I am only implementing your instructions, my lord,' Max replied, with all the fake devotion of a henchman.

Darkos, still seething, was at a loss for words.

'We'll make an exception for tonight! A special reopening!' he yelled, loud enough to break even the strongest eardrums.

Max took a slow look around.

'Okay,' he said calmly.

Easylow reconnected the battery and the lights came back on, revealing a pile of henchmen in the middle of the dance floor. It resembled a rugby match riot that had ended badly.

Darkos advanced. 'Now at last I have you, Selenia. Your little quest is over.'

The pile began to sort itself out as best it could. The last henchmen to emerge were somewhat ragged, but they were proudly carrying their three prisoners, trussed from head to foot.

Darkos looked at the prisoners and his face darkened with fury.

They had accidentally tied up three henchmen. Our heroes were gone.

'That blasted little princess!' Darkos looked as if he might explode.

'FIND THEM!' he roared.

Chapter 18

Darkos's voice echoed down into the basement, where our three heroes were hiding.

'Did you hear that?' Betameche shuddered. 'He sounds monstrous!'

'I hope that Max and his friends won't be punished because of us,' said the princess.

'You don't have to worry about them,' said Arthur. 'I'm sure Max can talk his way out of anything!'

Selenia sighed. She didn't like running away, but she knew Arthur was right.

'Come on! Time is passing and we have a mission!' Arthur said, taking her arm. Selenia let herself be pulled, and our three heroes took off into the darkness.

For quite some time they followed the oozing, dull, blue-green edge that bordered an interminable concrete wall. Finally they arrived at a sort of gigantic plaque on the ground, made of cast iron. Selenia knelt beside a hole in the centre of it.

It was not very big – hardly big enough to pass through. The walls were muddy and looked as if they descended for ever.

'There. It's there,' said Selenia.

'What's there?' replied Arthur, hoping she wasn't saying what he thought she was saying.

'The direct route, one way, to Necropolis,' Selenia explained, staring into the bottomless hole. 'This is where the unknown really begins. No Minimoy has ever returned safely from that nightmare city. So you should both think very carefully before following me,' the princess said gravely.

The three friends looked at one another in silence. Each was thinking about the amazing adventures they had already experienced and wondering how much worse it could get.

Arthur met Selenia's eyes and she forced a brave smile. He slowly extended his hand over the hole.

'My future is tied to yours, Selenia. And so my future is at your side.'

She put her hand in Arthur's.

Betameche placed his hand on top of theirs.

Our three heroes thus sealed their pact. They would go to the end together, for better or worse.

'By the grace of the gods!' said the princess solemnly.

'By the grace of the gods!' the two boys echoed in unison.

Selenia took a deep breath and leaped into the hole. Betameche held his nose and followed his sister without pausing to think. The hole swallowed him up in turn.

Arthur was still for a moment, thinking that this well swallowed bodies like quicksand. Then he took a deep breath and jumped feet first into the hole.

'It's you and me, Maltazard!' he cried before disappearing into the night and the mud.

Once again he had pronounced the cursed name.

Let us hope that, this time, it will bring him better luck.

To be continued . . .